HIKING TRAILS OF CAPE BRETON

Also by Michael Haynes
Hiking Trails of Nova Scotia, 7th edition

HIKING TRAILS OF

CAPE BRETON

MICHAEL HAYNES

HOSTELLING INTERNATIONAL — NOVA SCOTIA

GOOSE LANE EDITIONS

Cover photograph © Peter Oickle, Atlantic Canada Nature Safaris, 1997. Inset photo of the Cape Breton Highlands, provided by Enterprise Cape Breton Corporation.
Author photograph taken at Victoria Park, Truro, by John Haynes.
Maps prepared with the assistance of Navitrak Engineering.
Cover and interior design by Ryan Astle.
Edited by Darrell Mesheau.
Printed in Canada by Transcontinental Printing.
10 9 8 7 6 5 4 3 2 1

Canadian Cataloguing in Publication Data
    Haynes, Michael, 1955-
    Hiking Trails of Cape Breton

Includes bibliographical references and index.
ISBN 0-86492-233-7

1. Trails — Nova Scotia — Cape Breton Island — Guidebooks.
2. Hiking — Nova Scotia — Cape Breton Island — Guidebooks.
3. Cape Breton Island (N.S.) — Guidebooks.   I. Title

GV199.44.C2H39 1999   796.5'1'097169   C99-950043-0

Published with the financial support of the Government of Canada, through the Book Publishing Industry Development Program, and the New Brunswick Department of Economic Development, Tourism and Culture.

Goose Lane Editions   Canadä
469 King Street
Fredericton, New Brunswick
CANADA E3B 1E5

CONTENTS

FOREWORD

I am pleased to have the opportunity to introduce *Hiking Trails of Cape Breton*, the first part of the 8th edition of *Hiking Trails of Nova Scotia*. The second part, *Hiking Trails of Mainland Nova Scotia*, will be completed in 2001.

Hostelling has had a close association with outdoor activities since its inception in the early years of this century. In fact, Richard Schirrmann, a German school-teacher, established the first hostel in order to provide an inexpensive place for young people to stay while they explored the countryside. As one might expect, walking was a popular activity with the first hostellers, just as it is today in many countries around the world.

Hostelling International — Nova Scotia (HI-NS) is carrying on a long-established tradition of encouraging outdoor pursuits. Since its founding in 1938, HI-NS (then known as the Canadian Youth Hostels Association — Nova Scotia Division) has offered an outdoor program consisting of such activities as hiking, bicycling, canoeing, and cross-country skiing for its members. In the early 1970s, the Association realized that there was a need for a publication which would provide information on hiking trails throughout Nova Scotia, not only for its members but for many others who wanted to explore the province on foot. Thus, with the financial assistance of the Nova Scotia Sport and Recreation Commission, the first edition of *Hiking Trails of Nova Scotia* was published. (Although this was the first edition of *HTNS*, we know that there was at least one earlier publication, printed in 1961 by HI-NS, which gave brief descriptions of a number of routes suitable for exploration on foot or bicycle or by canoe.)

As soon as the first edition was printed, it became apparent that the work had really only just begun, because new trails were being established, old ones, unfortunately, were abandoned, and legislative changes had profound effects on trail development. Hikers are fortunate that interest in maintaining current information has been sustained for more than twenty-five years.

To those of you who have been using *Hiking Trails of Nova Scotia* over the years, it is hardly necessary to explain why one explores the countryside on foot. But for those who are considering such an activity for the first time, it may be useful to consider this question for a moment or two. I believe that there are many reasons why one would hike along a trail. There is the physical challenge to complete a task which we have accepted; there is the desire to maintain a level of fitness; there is the opportunity to see the natural beauty around us; there is the need to escape from the stress and demands put upon us by everyday living and working; and there is the very personal need for us to find out more about ourselves through communion with nature. Some of these reasons may be more important to some than others; some may become more important in the future than they are now; while others will decline in stature. However, we can be sure that the need to explore our world on foot will always exist, and we will all benefit from satisfying that need. I congratulate Hostelling International — Nova Scotia for helping make it possible for us to hike the trails of Nova Scotia.

Dave Horne
Executive Director, HI-NS (1972-1981)

PREFACE

Much has changed in the outdoor community since I first started writing about Nova Scotia trails in 1994. Interest in the outdoors, and in hiking in particular, has increased steadily in that time. Consequently, the number of people on the more popular trails has grown considerably, forcing those desiring solitude onto more remote byways. Fortunately, the demand is being met through initiatives such as the Trans Canada Trail and by community associations that are planning and building new walking and hiking trails from one end of the province to the other. The provincial government in late 1998 announced $1.5 million of new funding, available through the economic diversification agreement with the federal government, to develop special scenic and coastal hikes, and another $500,000 for the Trans Canada Trail. More than ever before, as we begin to recognize exactly how special our province is, new trails are becoming a priority of the Nova Scotia tourism industry.

I have changed as well, learning, I hope, from the many comments of enthusiastic Nova Scotians who have told me about their favourite hiking trail or telephoned me after one of my CBC *Information Morning* commentaries to answer a question I had asked about plants or animals. Further, in addition to my increased knowledge of the back paths of the province, I have developed a deepening appreciation for the tiny peninsula and islands on which we live. They truly are remarkable. I am constantly surprised by the beauty I find on so many of these trails. Cape Breton is an endless treasure trove of spectacular scenery, so much so that it is no wonder we so often take it for granted.

Whether you hike, bike, snowmobile, or just drive your car, please explore this province. There is more here than you can possibly imagine.

Michael Haynes
May, 1999

INTRODUCTION

Attempting to describe the beauty of Cape Breton Island is an ill-advised exercise. The steep-sided coastal slopes north of Cheticamp, the long, deserted sandy beaches below Cape Gabarus, the eerie shapes of stunted balsam fir on the highlands plateau taiga: each is very different, yet all evoke awe and wonderment from hundreds of thousands of people every year. Many try to explain what they have seen; there are hundreds of accounts from visitors, the famous and the humble, that strive to portray the emotion roused by the raw splendor of this rugged island, and there are dozens of books devoted to capturing the essence of its haunted landscape in extraordinary photographs. Yet, in the end, the most poignant testimonial to Cape Breton's captivating influence may be the plain words of a life-long resident of one of the island's tiny, remote villages, who says, "I can't imagine ever living anywhere else."

Situated at the northeastern corner of Nova Scotia, separated physically from the rest of the province by the narrow Strait of Canso, Cape Breton Island is a magical place, where the unique is somehow ordinary. Approximately 150 km (93 mi) at its longest and 100 km (62 mi) at its widest, Cape Breton covers slightly more than 10,000 km^2 (3850 mi^2) of land area and enjoys more than 2000 km (1200 mi) of ocean coastline. The rocks making up its fabled Highlands are the oldest in the province; its hills are the highest. The varied topography of the island contains portions of three different continents: North America, South America, and Africa. More unusual orchids and other plants can be found on Cape Breton than anywhere else in Nova Scotia, and if you do not see at least one moose, you have not been looking.

Hiking Trails of Cape Breton contains details of more than 50 trails and 560 km (350 mi) of walking, and is, I hope, a worthwhile successor to the fondly remembered *Walk Cape Breton*, printed in 1975. I have attempted to find and include entries from every corner of the island, interior and coastline, highlands and lowlands, to balance the selections. Further, I have tried to provide a broad range of choice based on the ability of the walker. Some of the trails are suitable for novices, while others should be attempted only by the more experienced. Each type will be clearly indicated, with the reasons for my recommendation stated.

Many of the entries are located in provincial and national parks; these tend to be the highest quality trails, well maintained and signed, with special maps and background information. However, many of the hiking opportunities presented in this book are unimproved: abandoned rail-lines, coastal walks following game trails, and deserted roads leading to forgotten farms. Unlike the park trails, few of these possess signage or services of any kind. But whatever the hike may be, I believe that you will find it worthy of inclusion in a collection of trails.

New Features

Hiking Trails of Cape Breton presents two important innovations to conventional hiking guides. Each trail description includes the Global Positioning System (GPS) co-ordinates for the principal trail access point, the *Start/ Parking*, as it is labelled on the accompanying map.

Not only will this new information provide a correct safety bearing for anyone with a GPS unit, but including GPS co-ordinates will also ease finding the start of unmarked trails and woods roads for the many users of this rapidly increasing, convenient, and affordable technology. As far as I know, *Hiking Trails of Cape Breton* is the first published guidebook to include this data as part of its standard information for every trail.

The second important feature is a Cell Phone Coverage section with each trail description. Like GPS units, cellular telephones are increasingly being carried by hikers as a safety device. Unfortunately, people often expect their phones to operate without confirming coverage details before they start their treks. Coverage is not always available, particularly in some of the more remote or geologically difficult areas of Cape Breton. In addition, at some sites the signal is too weak for lower-powered phones. By including this information, I hope to prevent hikers' discovering that their phones do not work at a critical time.

Trans Canada Trail

Since 1992, the concept of developing a multi-use recreational corridor stretching across the country has gradually been transformed from a dream to near-reality. On its official opening date, September 9, 2000, the Trans Canada Trail Foundation, the provincial trail associations, and the community trail-building organizations hope to have a route available for its five core uses — cross-country skiing, snowmobiling, horseback riding, bicycling, and hiking — from Newfoundland to British Columbia to the Northwest Territories. The Trans Canada Trail will be the longest trail in the world and one of the largest volunteer projects ever achieved.

On Cape Breton Island, the path of the Trans Canada Trail will extend from North Sydney, where the ferry from Newfoundland docks, to the Canso Causeway, the land connection with the mainland. In 1998, when I did the field research for this book, much of the route of the trail was selected, but construction had not been completed. However, two hikes profiled in the text, the Ceilidh Coastal Trail and Mabou Rail Trail, are both sections of what will be the final path of the Trans Canada Trail, and both are available for use.

I hope you enjoy *Hiking Trails of Cape Breton* and find that the information in it helps you to appreciate fully this remarkable gem of the Maritimes, Cape Breton Island.

How to Use This Book

Hiking Trails of Cape Breton is not a comprehensive list of all the trails on the island. For the purposes of this book, I have divided Cape Breton into five regions: Cape Breton Highlands National Park and four others conforming to the corners of the island. In each of these regions I tried to ensure variety by selecting ten hiking trails: some coastal, some inland, a few easy, one or two more challenging, and through both hills and lowlands. This occasionally meant that I had to leave out a very good trail because I had selected another, similar hike in the same region, or because I had to include a trail principally because it provided the necessary variety for that region. The selection was mine alone; if I left out your favourite trail, please let me know.

Every region begins with a brief introduction, including a map indicating the approximate starting points of the trails. Each trail description is a separate essay, incorporating a reproduction of the most recent topo-

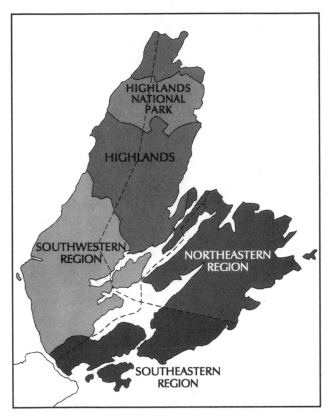

CAPE BRETON ISLAND

graphical map of the area, scaled to fit the book's pages, and with the trail route superimposed upon it. Every trail is described using the same basic format:

Name of Trail (sometimes my own invention)

Length: gives return-trip distance in kilometres (and miles), rounded to the nearest half-kilometre (and quarter-mile).

Hiking Time: based on an average walker's rate of 4 km (2.5 mi) per hour. Do not assume that this accurately reflects the amount of time you will require to complete any particular hike until you can compare your time with that of the book. Each person sets his or her own pace, which will vary according to weather conditions, length of the trail, and fitness level.

Type of Trail: indicating the footing that will be encountered.

Uses: including hiking, biking, cross-country skiing, horseback riding, snowmobiling, and driving ATVs.

Facilities: telling whether services such as washrooms or water will be found on the trail.

Gov't Topo Map: the designation of the national topographic map of the terrain covered by the trail.

Rating: a designation from 1 to 5, with 1 being suitable for all fitness and experience levels and 5 being recommended for experienced and very fit outdoor people only. These ratings are my own opinion based on consideration of length, elevation change, condition of the treadway, and signage. If you are a novice, choose level 1 and 2 hikes initially, and work your way up as you gain experience. Starting at level 4 or 5 will only ensure that your hiking career includes punishment from the beginning. All level 4 and 5 hikes, and a few others, include a brief indication of the characteristics that give these trails a higher rating.

Trailhead GPS Reference: the latitude and longitude of the start/finish of the hike. This data was collected using a GARMIN GPS 12XL Receiver and was not corrected. It may therefore be inaccurate by 100-200 m/yd.

Each trail outline is divided into the following sections:

Access Information: how to get to the starting point from a community easily found on the basic Nova Scotia Tourism road map.

Introduction: background about the trail, including historical, natural, and geographical information, as well as my personal observations or recommendations.

Trail Description: a walk-through of the hike, relating what I found when I last travelled this route. In every case I describe junctions and landmarks from the perspective of someone following the trail in the direction I have indicated. If travelling in the opposite direction, remember to reverse my bearings.

Cautionary Notes: hunting season, cliffs, high winds, raging seas, or anything I believe you should be cautious about. Please take these warnings seriously, for everybody's sake. An accident in the wilderness is more dangerous than one in the city simply because of the remoteness from rapid assistance.

Cell Phone Coverage: how well a cellular phone will

work on this trail, including locations of dead spots. The data was collected using a Motorola StarTAC 6000e phone supplied by MTT Mobility. If this particular phone was able to send and receive calls, any mobile telephone should do at least as well. New cell phone tower construction will mean better coverage in the future for many of these trails.

Future Plans: what, if anything, is intended in the way of changes to the trail or park in the next few years.

Further Information: a separate brochure is available for many trails, particularly those in parks. I will mention these here, and a list of addresses from which brochures and other information are available is included in the back of the book.

In addition, the Trails at a Glance chart on pages 24-25 shows the length and degree of difficulty of all the trails.

Equipment

The recreation industry produces excellent specialized equipment for the outdoors person, with the selection growing every year. I cannot provide recommendations about specific brands; each person must discover what works best for him or her. However, there are a few items that should always be carried whenever we enter the forest, even if only for a short hike. Doing so may help ensure that every hiking experience is an enjoyable and safe one.

Few people know that, by law, you must carry matches, knife, and compass when you travel in the woods in Nova Scotia. You are also required to know how to use the compass, something surprisingly few people can actually do, although most municipal recreation departments offer courses in map and compass reading. Proper footwear is essential and should be selected with care. Other items are indispensable, and I believe you should always include them, even in the summer:

Map: I always carry a map when I go hiking. Is it swampy? Are there cliffs? Are houses nearby? If I get lost, what direction do I follow to find people? In provincial and federal parks, a special map of the trail is often available. Otherwise, I purchase the National Topographic System of Canada 1:50 000 scale map of the area. A map gives you a sense of the terrain you will be hiking through.

Water: Perhaps nothing is more important than water. You can live up to two weeks without food; you may die in as few as three days without water. I carry one litre per person on a hike up to 10 km (6 mi), and more if the distance is greater, if the day is particularly hot or humid, or if I am taking children with me. Dehydration occurs rapidly while hiking, and the accompanying headache or dizziness diminishes the pleasure of the experience. Drink small sips of water often, and do not wait until you are thirsty to do so.

Food: Though not really necessary on a day hike, I always carry something to snack on while I walk. Apples, trail mix, bagels — anything like this is good. Chocolate bars, chips, and other junk food are not the best choice for several reasons, but better something than nothing.

Whistle: If you get lost and want to attract attention, a whistle will be heard far better than your voice and is less likely to wear out from continuous use. If you don't believe that, take one outside the house and give a couple of blasts. See how much attention you attract.

First Aid Kit: When you are out in the woods, even little problems suddenly become very important. A small first aid kit with Band-Aids, gauze, tape, moleskin, etc., permits you to deal with blisters and bruises that might require attention.

Garbage Bag: You should always carry your own trash out with you: food wrappers, juice bottles, and even apple cores should go into the bag. If you are hiking on a well-used trail, you will always find litter left behind by others. Take a moment to put as much as you can into your own garbage bag. If you don't do it, it probably will not get done.

Warm Sweater and/or Rain Jacket: Cape Breton weather is highly changeable, and forecasts are often not accurate for the Highlands or the coastline. Rain and wind combine for uncomfortable, possibly life-threatening, conditions. No matter how good the weather seems to be, always carry some heavier clothing, particularly in spring and fall.

Backpack: You need something to carry all this, and I recommend that you invest in a good quality day-pack. It should have adjustable shoulder straps, a waist strap, a large inner pouch, and roomy outer pockets. The items I have listed will fit easily inside a good pack and will sit comfortably on your back. After one or two trips, wearing it will become just another part of your walking routine. In fact, I never hike without my pack.

Optional (but recommended) Equipment: sunscreen, hat, bug repellent, camera, binoculars, field guides, toilet paper, writing paper, and pen.

Really Optional Equipment: extra socks, tarp, rope,

eating utensils, flashlight, towel, bathing suit, small stove, fuel, toothbrush, toothpaste, soap, and sleeping bag.

Hazards

There are few dangerous plants and animals in Cape Breton. All four species of snake found here, for example, are harmless. But there are a few things to remember before you enter the woods.

Weather: High winds along the coast are common, and the Highlands have the harshest environment in the Maritimes. The wind chill factor can become significant, even in late spring and early fall. For example, you might start hiking inland at a temperature of +16°C (61°F). Reaching the coast, winds gust to 60 kph (37 mph). The wind chill equivalent becomes +6°C (43°F). If wind chill combines with water chill from ocean spray, fog, or rain, hypothermia becomes probable. Carrying sweaters and rain gear is always a good idea.

Conditions in the Highlands are unpredictable and highly variable. Be prepared for any type of weather, regardless of forecasts.

Bears: Black bears live in Cape Breton, although they are rarely sighted. Parks Canada has an excellent brochure that I recommend obtaining. It says that, if a bear approaches, do not try to run away or climb a tree. Black bears do both better and faster than people and will react to you as food attempting to escape. Instead, keep your face turned toward the bear while avoiding direct eye contact, and slowly back away from it. If the bear charges, scream, yell, and kick at it, which may frighten it away. You may instead drop your pack and hope it distracts the bear. If neither of these manoeuvres works, the best bet is to lie on the ground in a fetal position, with arms drawn up to protect your face and neck, and attempt to remain still, however frightening and painful it might be. Most bears will be content to hit a person a few times, then withdraw.

Cougars: Although rumoured to live in Nova Scotia, none has yet been photographed, trapped, or shot.

Lynx: Largely restricted to the Highlands, their principal diet is snowshoe hare, and they are very wary of humans.

Moose: These are extremely common in Cape Breton, especially in the Highlands. Dawn and dusk are the times they are most likely to wander onto the road. Bulls weigh up to 650 kg (1400 lb) and can knock a car off the highway. They can be unpredictable, especially during the fall rutting season. Moose are not just larger deer; treat them with as much respect and caution as you would bear.

Hunting Season: Hunting is permitted in many of the areas covered in this book. Usually starting in early October, hunting season varies from year to year for different types of game. Contact the Department of Natural Resources for detailed information before going into the woods in the fall. No hunting is allowed on Sunday, but always wear a bright orange garment for safety nevertheless.

Poison Ivy: While relatively uncommon in Cape Breton, it may be encountered on some coastal dunes and in a few other places.

Ticks: There are no ticks in Cape Breton.

The Margaree Valley near Portree.

Trail Name	1	2	3	4	5	km (mi)	page
TRAILS AT A GLANCE							
	Difficulty Level						
CAPE BRETON HIGHLANDS NATIONAL PARK							
L'Acadien				X		10 (6.25)	30
Benjies Lake & Bog Trail	X					3.5 (2.25); 1 (.5)	34
Le Chemin du Buttereau		X				7 (4.25)	39
Coastal and Jigging Cove					X	19 (11.75)	43
Fishing Cove				X		15 (9.5)	47
Franey			X			7.5 (4.75)	53
Glasgow Lakes			X			9.5 (6)	59
MacIntosh Brook	X					3 (1.75)	62
Skyline		X				7 (4.25)	66
Warren Lake		X				6 (3.75)	70
HIGHLANDS							
Cabots Landing Provincial Park	X					7 (4.25)	79
Cape Smokey Provincial Park			X			11 (6.75)	83
Englishtown			X			10 (6.25)	89
Meat Cove				X		16 (10)	93
Money Point				X		16 (10)	99
North River Provincial Park					X	18 (11.25)	103
Portree - Big Intervale			X			8 (5)	109
Tenerife Mountain				X		4 (2.5)	113
Usige Ban Falls Provincial Park	X					7 (4.25)	117
White Point		X				6 (3.75)	121
NORTHEASTERN							
Cape Breton					X	18 (11.25)	131
Cape Percé		X				8.5 (5.25)	134
East Bay Hills					X	26 (16.25)	139
Fairy Hole			X			4.5 (2.75)	145
Gabarus - Belfry Gut					X	40 (25)	150

Trail Name	Difficulty Level					km (mi)	page
	1	2	3	4	5		
Kennington Cove			X			8 (5)	155
Lighthouse Point				X		14.5 (9)	161
Mira River Provincial Park	X					6.5 (4)	167
Provincial Parks: Ben Eoin, Dalem Lake, Petersfield	X					1.5 (1); 2.5 (1.5); 2 (1.25)	170
Two Rivers Wildlife Park	X					5 (3)	177
SOUTHEASTERN							
Cape Auguet					X	23 (14.5)	185
Cape George	X					4 (2.5)	189
Capelin Cove				X		17 (10.5)	193
Delorier Island		X				9 (5.5)	199
Lennox Passage Provincial Park	X					4 (2.5)	204
Little River Reservoir			X			9 (5.5)	209
Point Michaud Provincial Park		X				12 (7.5)	213
Port Hawkesbury		X				8 (5)	219
Pringle Mountain			X			13.5 (8.5)	223
St. Peters Rail Trail – Battery Provincial Park		X				14 (8.75)	227
SOUTHWESTERN							
Broad Cove		X				13.5 (8.5)	237
Ceilidh Coastal Trail				X		31 (19.5)	241
Highland Hill		X				7.5 (4.75)	247
Mabou Highlands – Beinn Bhiorach			X			10.5 (6.5)	253
Mabou Highlands Loop				X		16 (10)	257
Mabou Rail Trail				X		24 (15)	262
Marble Mountain		X				11.5 (7.25)	269
Pipers Glen – Egypt Falls				X		14 (8.75)	273
Strathlorne Forestry Complex	X					4.5 (2.75)	278
Whycocomagh Provincial Park		X				2.5 (1.5)	282

The Cheticamp River from the Trous de Saumon Trail. L'Acadien Trail provides views from the steep ridges above the river.

CAPE BRETON HIGHLANDS
NATIONAL PARK

The Cape Breton Highlands must have been the obvious choice as the location of the first national park in Nova Scotia. Cut by innumerable little bays and inlets, the land rises steeply out of the ocean to create a plateau over 450 m (1500 ft) high featuring the only taiga region in the Maritimes. The coastline itself consists of spectacular sandy beaches, rocky capes, and rugged headlands jutting into the Atlantic. So, when offered a choice between this and sites in Yarmouth County and the Cape Blomidon area in Kings County, the highlands location was strongly recommended by Park Service inspectors. In 1936, 1186 km² (741 m²) of land in the northern parts of Inverness and Victoria counties were incorporated into the Cape Breton Highlands National Park. Subsequent reductions for hydroelectric power projects on the southern boundary near the Cheticamp and Ingonish rivers brought the park to its present size, 950.5 km² (594 m²).

Active in both summer and winter recreation, the park contains three large and three small camping areas and one wilderness campground. Almost 200 km (125 mi) of hiking is available on 27 different signed and maintained trails, and mountain biking is permitted on the Clyburn Valley, Lake of Islands, and Trous de Saumon paths. In winter, the extremely heavy snowfall permits cross-country skiing almost everywhere. In addition to these more rugged activities, the park also maintains an 18-hole golf course, Highland Links, near Keltic Lodge at Ingonish Beach.

Main park entrances are at Ingonish on the east coast and Cheticamp on the west, and information centres with nature bookstores can be found at either side. Fees are charged to drive through the park on the Cabot Trail, and in 1999 the rate for an adult was $3.50 for one day, $10.50 for four days, and $17.50 for the year. The best buy was the $30 adult Atlantic Regional National Park Pass, valid in Cape Breton Highlands, Kejimkujik, Prince Edward Island, Fundy, Kouchibouguac, Terra Nova, and Gros Morne national parks from June to October. Camping charges in 1999 varied from $15/day for wilderness sites to $21/day for sites with electricity, water, and sewer. Fees vary depending upon age, length of stay, group composition, and services used. Contact Cape Breton Highlands National Park, Ingonish Beach, Nova Scotia B0C 1L0, or telephone (902) 285-2691 or (902) 224-3403 for a complete list of rates.

This park contains some of the most stunning scenery in the province and is justly a primary destination for many tourists. The hikes I have featured include a portion of every landscape: coastline, mountain, valley, headland, and plateau, but many more options are available. This is also one of the least populated areas of Nova Scotia, far from large towns. Your chances of meeting wildlife, such as moose, are greater in the park than anywhere else in Cape Breton. Be prepared for the wild and the rugged.

No hunting is permitted within the boundaries of the national park.

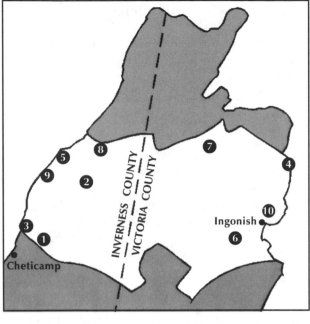

Cheticamp
INVERNESS COUNTY
VICTORIA COUNTY
Ingonish

CAPE BRETON HIGHLANDS NATIONAL PARK

L'Acadien

Length: 10 km (6.25 mi) return

Time: 3-4 hr

Type: walking path, former road

Rating (1-5): 4 (steep)

Uses: hiking

Facilities: outhouses, campsite, firewood, showers, shelters, picnic tables, garbage cans, water

Gov't Topo Map: Cheticamp River 11 K/10

Trailhead GPS Reference: N 46° 38" 48.8' W 60° 56" 59.4'

Access Information: The trailhead is located across the road from the Park Information Centre at the western entry to the park. Look for the trailhead map sign by the forest edge near the highway.

Introduction: As soon as you enter Cape Breton Highlands National Park, the Information Centre comes into view on your right. Take a few moments to explore its many fascinating visual displays and its ten-minute slide presentation. Spend even more time in Les Amis du Plein Air Bookstore, which is bulging with maps, books, and information that will help you become familiar with northern Cape Breton's enticing wilderness area. Park entry permits, camping permits, and fishing licences can be purchased at the centre.

Cheticamp Campground is open throughout the year, and several hiking/cross-country skiing trails begin here. This is a tremendous outdoor recreational resource that is often full in July and August and barely used in other months. Winter camping can be made easier by the restaurants only a five-minute drive away.

L'Acadien is a challenging hike that requires climbing from near sea level to 365 m (1200 ft). On hot summer days you must carry sufficient water or you will have a

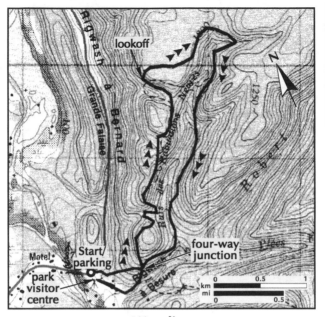

L'Acadien

very unpleasant experience. On the other hand, the panorama of the Cheticamp shore and the Gulf of St. Lawrence from the higher viewing platforms will be worth the exertion. Those desiring an easier ascent should reverse the direction I outline.

Trail Description: As soon as you enter the forest the trail begins to climb – get used to it! The wide cart track threads its way for about 500 m/yd through the thick white spruce that is reclaiming former farmlands before it reaches a four-way trail junction at the base of the loop. A bench is available for resting should you require it. Signs indicate the route options. Take the left path and continue up the hill through the thick spruce. In the first clearing you reach, on your left, there are ruins of an old homestead. Benches are available to enjoy the view of Cheticamp Island to the southwest.

About 50 m/yd beyond this point you reach another junction, where you also find an outhouse. The trail heading right continues up a knoll to end at a lookoff. The main trail heads left, however, and becomes a narrow footpath as it climbs the steeper slope. Watch for little lookoffs on your left. Be cautious. There are no guard-rails, and the hillside is sheer, but it offers a view from high above the Rigwash à Bernard and Melane's Pond.

The trees change to mostly hardwoods as your el-evation increases, and as you scramble up the slope several benches are provided for rests. The path moves across the hill and follows the interior slope for some time, providing views of the steep ridges separating Robert Brook from the Cheticamp River. Maple, ash, and beech trees, some quite old, shelter in little vales, providing shade as you toil uphill and as the treadway becomes covered by grasses.

Characteristic of the highlands, the top of the ridge is fairly broad and rounded and broken into several small summits. Near the crest your climb becomes more gradual, and you even lose elevation when you move between the small hilltops. Vegetation changes as well; the trees are much smaller and show the effects of wind and exposure. The original forests were cleared for pasture by the Acadian settlers, and since that clearing, disease has killed many of the softwoods. If you look at the neighbouring hillsides you will see many bare patches. The view, how-ever, is incredible. On your left is the ocean and to your right the steep-sided ravines of the highlands. View-ing stations become more frequent as you ascend, and the trail culminates at lookoff on the slope high above Rigwash à Bernard facing in the direction of Cheticamp Island. Every time I have walked this trail I have en-countered someone sitting there, quietly enjoying the sight.

From this final lookoff, the trail heads inland across the almost treeless plateau, initially still climbing. In summer the bushes grow quite thick and hide large rocks in the treadway. Soon you notice you are losing elevation, and within minutes the deep ravine of the Ruisseau des Habitations Neuves cuts across your route. The trail works left, heading downslope until it reaches the very end of the valley. The foliage of huge hardwoods shades you again as the trail cuts sharply right, contouring along the slope. Ravine walls tower on both sides, and the path follows the creek as it descends toward the Cheticamp River. Bridges with guardrails, frequent and sturdy and too numerous to count, move the path back and forth across the brook, and benches are available for the weary.

After approximately 3 km (2 mi) following the brook, the track moves away and climbs the right-hand slope. Newly built, this path cuts through thick white spruce and still has a treadway that is mostly dirt and rock. In about 500 m/yd, you return to the four-way junction you encountered early in the hike. Turn left, heading steeply downhill to meet Robert Brook, a wide, active stream, and follow it until you emerge from the trees next to a park maintenance building about 500 m/yd later. To return to your car, walk around the building and follow the road to the Information Centre.

Cautionary Notes: Bears are frequently reported, eating the strawberries in early summer and the blueberries later in the season.

The tops of the hills are quite open and exposed to the high winds common to the Cheticamp area. Be prepared for extreme conditions, especially in spring and fall.

Cell Phone Coverage: Once you reach the first junction, you should be able to receive a strong signal until you begin your descent into the Ruisseau des Habitations

Neuves ravine. No calls can be made on the back part of the hike at all, until you have almost completed the loop. The cell signal is also very weak at sea level near the Park Administration Centre and the trailhead.

Further Information: Ask at Les Amis du Plein Air bookstore at the Park Information Centre for greater detail about the Acadian settlement, the geology, and the natural history of this region. Parks Canada produces several brochures, including a hiking route pamphlet, and this trail is indicated on their special topographical map of the park. All can be obtained at the information centres at Cheticamp and Ingonish.

Benjies Lake & Bog Trail

Length: 3.5 km (2.25 mi) + 1 km (.5 mi) return

Time: 1 hr

Trail: former road, walking paths, boardwalks

Rating (1-5): 1

Uses: hiking, cross-country skiing

Facilities: garbage cans, outhouses

Gov't Topo Map: Cheticamp River 11 K/10
Trailhead GPS References: N 46° 44" 51.1' W 60° 49" 19.0' (Benjies Lake); N 46° 44" 29.6' W 60° 49" 39.8' (Bog Trail)

Access Information: From the west park entrance north of Cheticamp, drive 19 km (11.75 mi) north on the Cabot Trail. Watch for the Bog Trail sign on your left, and turn left off the road into the parking area. The entrance to the Benjies Lake Trail is 800 m/yd further north. Its parking area is on the left of the road, with the trailhead on the opposite side of the highway.

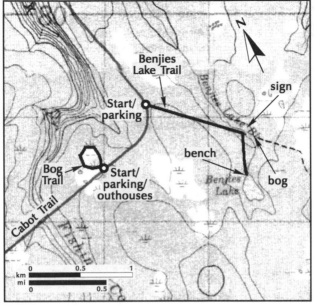

Benjies Lake & Bog Trail

Introduction: When people think of animals of the highlands, they think of moose. The largest mammals in Nova Scotia, weighing up to 650 kg (1400 lb), moose seem to prefer higher elevations. When spruce budworm killed most of the balsam fir that covered these hills in the 1970s, young shrubs grew up in their place. With this abundant food supply, the moose population has grown very large. In one hour at dawn in August 1998, I saw 15 calves, cows, and bulls on the top of North Mountain, less than 25 km (16 mi) away. Benjies Lake is an excellent spot to sight moose at any time of day.

The shortest trail in the national park, Bog Trail is also the most heavily used. Through the aid of interpretative panels, you will learn more about the fascinating environment of the highlands than on any other trail.

Completely boardwalked, it traces a short circle through a sloped fen on the top of the highland plateau. Frequent panels provide information about the geology, climate, and plant and animal life of this unique location. Wheelchair accessible, it can be enjoyed by everybody, but it is a worthwhile stop for even the most experienced hiker.

These trails are quite close to each other, the trailheads about 800 m/yd apart. Leaving your car at one spot and walking both will mean a hike of slightly less than 6 km (4 mi).

Trail Description: The Benjies Lake Trail starts across the road from its parking area and down the bank of the highway. The entrance is well signed, and once you begin your hike along the old fire road, the trail is almost perfectly straight for the first kilometre. Fairly wide and dry, it climbs gently for the first few hundred metres before beginning a slightly steeper descent down to Benjies Lake Brook. Look closely in the softwood around you. Broad moose paths lead in every direction, and you're likely to find moose in the middle of the path.

Turn right when you reach two benches and a sign. The fire road continues deep into the interior, and cross-country skiers use it to traverse the highlands in the late winter. But the rest of the year it is quite boggy and difficult and not recommended for the average day-hiker.

In the final 500 m/yd of the trail, boardwalks cross the frequent wet areas. More of a footpath now, the trail passes through thick stands of balsam fir that close in tightly on both sides. When the lake becomes visible through the trees, slow down. If there are any moose, you do not wish to startle them. Cautiously advance along the final boardwalk, past the last trees, and quietly seat yourself on the bench by the water's edge. This is the end of the trail, and even if there are no animals at the

The boardwalk along the Bog Trail.

lake, this is a wonderful place to sit and enjoy the tranquillity of the highland plateau. When ready, return along the same path.

The Bog Trail is located on the French Mountain Bog, 410 m (1350 ft) above sea level. A large parking area accommodates its many visitors, and there are public outhouses. The interpretative panels are arranged for a clockwise circuit, and painted "enter" and "exit" signs on the boardwalk direct traffic. Wide enough for two, with a raised border on either side, the boardwalk meanders around the low bog, skirting small ponds and passing between clumps of stunted tamarack and black spruce. Larger platforms have been constructed around the panels, permitting passage when two groups meet. The bog environment is extremely delicate, and it is very important to stay on the boardwalk at all times.

Take time to read the panels and to look around. This walk is a naturalist's delight, designed to be enjoyed slowly. The trees around you, barely head-high, are 50 or more years old, hardy survivors of this poorly drained and harsh environment. In spring, the profusion of orchids in these soggy grounds is amazing: leatherleaf, sheep laurel, bog rosemary, fringed orchis, and dragon's mouth being just a few of the species. But they are all tiny and mixed in with the thick grasses, so you must look carefully to find them.

At the far end of the boardwalk, a bench faces a pond. Sit and absorb the sights and sounds of this uncommon place. About 250 m/yd and several more panels remain; then you are back at the parking area.

Cautionary Notes: Up on the highland plateau the weather is the most variable and harsh of any in the Maritimes. You can start walking to Benjies Lake in warm sunshine and end up returning drenched by freezing rain, even in the summer! Be prepared.

While fairly reserved most of the year, male moose can become aggressive in the late fall. Do not attempt to approach too closely, and be prepared to back away if necessary.

Do not throw coins into the small ponds along the Bog Trail. The metal can be poisonous to pond life.

Cell Phone Coverage: I obtained no signal at all on either of the two trails.

Further Information: Parks Canada brochures on trails, flora, and fauna are available. David Lawley's book, *A Nature and Hiking Guide to Cape Breton's Cabot Trail,* outlines both of these walks.

Le Chemin du Buttereau

Length: 7 km (4.25 mi) return
Time: 2 hr
Type: walking path, former road
Rating (1-5): 2

Uses: hiking
Facilities: garbage cans

Gov't Topo Map: Cheticamp River 11 K/10
Trailhead GPS Reference: N 46° 39" 18.8' W 60° 56" 53.6'

Access Information: From the national park's western entrance, drive 1 km (.5 mi) north. Watch for the sign; the parking area is on the left beside Melane's Pond.

Introduction: This trail was once the only overland link between Cheticamp and the tiny community of Cap Rouge. Originally a cart track constructed by Acadian settlers in the late 1700s, the Buttereau Road was abandoned in the late 1930s when the present Cabot Trail was constructed. In 1985, the track was opened as a hiking trail to mark the hundredth anniversary of Canada's national park system.

The geological history of this area is fascinating. For example, the Cheticamp River used to flow down the current route of the Cabot Trail. During the last ice age, a dam of ice diverted the flow northward into its present course, leaving dry the Rigwash á Bernard, a 100-m (330-ft) deep gorge beneath the Grande Falaise.

This description is actually two trails joined into one hike. Le Chemin du Buttereau ends in the middle of the Le Buttereau loop. Combining the two provides a slightly longer hike and probably more accurately reflects what most people hike who start at the Le Chemin du Buttereau trailhead.

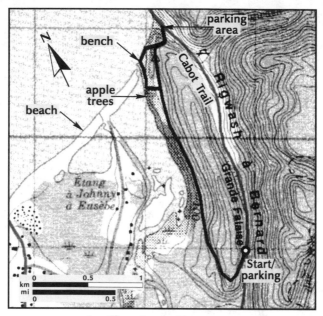

Le Chemin de Buttereau

Trail Description: The trailhead marker is located at the south end of the parking area, and the path enters the woods immediately, initially heading south. Perched on the side of a small but steep hill, the wide former cart track circles around its southern end to head almost due north. As it works its way around the base of the hill, it passes the edge of a small pond, which is home to a family of beaver. The tiny brook draining Melane's Pond is all that separates you from the entrance to Cheticamp Campground.

Climbing gradually at first, the trail nearly levels out once you are heading north on the western slope of the hill, and spruce trees form a dense, living ceiling for much of the first kilometre. A vibrant carpet of sphagnum moss lines either side. A few roots and rocks intrude, but the track is generally wide and quite easy walking.

As you continue along the nearly straight former road, you will find a few benches and viewing stations overlooking the beach at Petit Étang. You encounter some wet areas now, with boardwalks crossing them, and you may recognize the remains of old stone walls on both sides of the path. Just before reaching the junction with Le Buttereau, you will notice a field on your left with old apple trees growing throughout.

At the junction, continue straight. The trail widens considerably, a whole row of trees having recently been removed. At the next junction, turn right, and climb the fairly steep hill to reach the parking area of Le Buttereau at its base on the other side. Your reward for this ascent is a breathtaking view of the towering Grande Falaise as you reach the crest. Sit on one of the benches here and observe the older pink Precambrian granite perched on top of the younger black volcanic rocks from the Ordovician-Silurian era. If you wish, return to your car, about 2.5 km (1.5 mi) along the Cabot Trail through the Rigwash á Bernard.

Otherwise, return to the last junction and turn right. Much more open with fewer tall trees, the trail heads directly to the coastline, where a bench is positioned at the narrowest point at the mouth of the Cheticamp River. This is a delightful spot to sit and watch the waves roll onto the long, sandy shore opposite. In the summer this beach is a favourite gathering place for people from the neighbouring communities, and the sounds of their laughter will even drown out the sounds of the gulls. Expect to find osprey and bald eagles nearby as well, waiting to catch salmon as they navigate the shallow entrance to the Cheticamp River. During spawning season, you can sometimes see the fish jumping as they head upstream.

The footpath turns left into the trees just before reaching the bench, a little set of stairs climbing up the bank. This turn is well signed, and the trail passes through another thicket of white spruce before emerging into a commonly wet field, inadequately traversed by a boardwalk. Your route follows the river for a short distance, giving good views of the small body of water trapped by the barrier of Petit Étang beach. Turning away from the water back into the woods, the path soon arrives at another soggy field, where it is once again surfaced by boardwalk. At the far end you can see the curious wooden structure that marks the junction with Le Chemin du Buttereau. Turn right here, and follow the familiar path back to your car, about 2.5 km (1.5 mi) away.

Cautionary Notes: none

Cell Phone Coverage: A sufficient signal for a call can be obtained on the coastal stretches, but it weakens considerably when you move behind the hill into the Rigwash á Bernard. Weaker phones probably cannot work under the thicker vegetation or at either of the two trailheads.

Further Information: Ask at Les Amis du Plein Air bookstore at the park administrative centre for greater detail about both the Acadian settlement and the geology of this region.

Coastal and Jigging Cove

Length: 19 km (11.75 mi) return

Time: 6 hr

Type: walking path, cobble beach

Rating (1-5): 5 (distance)

Uses: hiking

Facilities: garbage cans, outhouses

Gov't Topo Map: Dingwall 11 K/16

Trailhead GPS Reference: N 46° 46" 42.6' W 60° 19" 55.9'

Access Information: The Coastal Trail can be picked up either at Halfway Brook, near Neils Harbour, from a parking lot next to the Cabot Trail, or at Black Brook Cove, which I will use as the starting point. Drive 20 km (12.5 mi) from the Ingonish information centre; the entrance to the beach and picnic site at Black Brook Cove is on your right, and it is well signed. Turn in there, then turn left at an intersection 100 m/yd in from the highway; the road ends in a parking lot.

Introduction: In July 1921, an out-of-control campfire started a blaze that devastated this area, destroying more than 1500 ha (3700 a) of forest. The situation was so serious that the communities of Neils Harbour and New Haven had to be evacuated by sea, with one ship being wrecked in the attempt. Contemporary reports state that "on the blackened coast, not a blade of grass remained." But the trees and plants returned quickly, in particular the usually scarce jack pine.

Jack pine is the rarest of three native pines found in Nova Scotia. Only two large stands are found inside the park, and this species is also uncommon elsewhere in Cape Breton. Able to grow on very poor soil, jack pines usually develop in pure stands. The seeds require

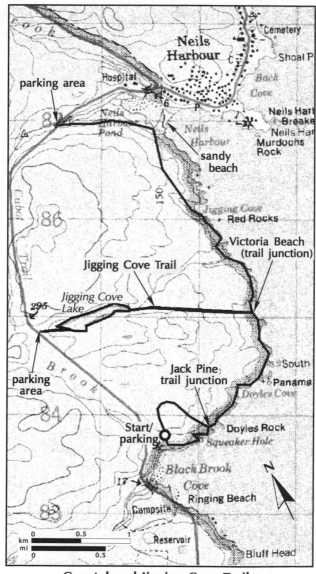

Coastal and Jigging Cove Trails

very high temperatures to germinate, 44°C (111°F), so a forest fire where seed trees are present can result in regeneration beneath a pure forest of jack pine. The woods along the Jack Pine Trail have been designated as a Heritage Tree Stand.

The Coastal Trail starts near the Black Brook beach and picnic area. Although only garbage cans are located at the trailhead, picnic tables and washrooms are found by the beach. Because of the presence of the Jack Pine and Jigging Cove trails, and the option of walking along the highway, this trail can be walked as either a 3 km (1.75 mi), 7 km (4.25 mi), or 19 km (11.75 mi) circuit. The Coastal Trail will provide some diversity to your highland itinerary.

Trail Description: The Coastal Trail begins at the lower (Ingonish) end of the parking lot (the Jack Pine Trail starts at the upper end). Descending into a deep ravine cut by a brook, the Coastal Trail immediately presents you with the chance to detour to a look-off viewing Black Brook Beach. The narrow main trail keeps left and winds through young softwoods, rising and falling as it accom-modates the rugged rocks near the coast. At several places in this first kilometre you will notice that flat stones have been arranged to create stairs. These enable people of most fitness levels to complete this portion of the Coastal Trail and return to the parking area along the Jack Pine Trail in 3 km (1.75 mi).

The junction with the Jack Pine Trail occurs just be-yond Squeaker Hole, a narrow cove that produces distinctive noises when waves hit it just right. Well signed, the Jack Pine Trail heads uphill and turns inland, but our route follows the ocean for now. For the next 1.5 km (1 mi) the well-defined trail continues to trace the waterline, occasionally dropping lower to cross sections of cobble beach. As you round a gently curving point, the first sight of Neils Harbour in the distance alerts you to the impending junction with the Jigging Cove trails.

As you cross the stones of Victoria Beach, the Jigging Cove Brook Trail joins from the woods on your left. Those interested in a longer hike should turn inland, as the path follows Jigging Cove Brook gently uphill to Jigging Cove Lake. Including this section in your hike adds a further 7 km (4.25 mi). A path has been constructed completely around this small body of water, and a 200 m/yd side-trail at the western end enables you to rejoin the highway. If you wish to return to your car, it is left about 2 km (1.25 mi) down the road. Moose are common in the lake and in the woods along the brook, especially at dawn and dusk. On a hot or windy day, the trees can provide welcome cover.

Continuing along the coast, you will find that the terrain gets rougher, forcing the trail to head into the woods. The coastline becomes more vertical, and when you reach Jigging Cove, about a kilometre beyond Victoria Beach, the path is forced to leave the shore and cut inland behind the roughest sections. This is the toughest part of the hike, climbing straight up almost from water level to above 30 m/yd, then descending to the sandbar separating Neils Harbour Pond from the ocean. You can walk along this sandy beach if you wish. A further kilometre remains as the trail follows the pond edge and Halfway Brook, crossing underneath the highway and ending in a parking lot, about 2 km (1.25 mi) from the community of Neils Harbour.

From here your choices are to return along the same path, hike back along the Cabot Trail to Black Brook Beach, or have someone pick you up. I recommend returning along the path. Even though this involves retracing the same ground, this is a beautiful walk and one of the very few coastal excursions available in the park. When you arrive at the junction with the Jack Pine Trail, follow it inland. Interpretative signs tell a fascinating story about nature and human intervention. It is worth the extra kilometre if you have the energy.

Cautionary Notes: There are several exposed fingers of land that jut into the ocean. Rogue waves, undetectable to most of us and most common during or just after a storm, can scour those points. Resist the temptation to stand at the very edge of the land with your toes in the water, except on calm days.

Cell Phone Coverage: Calls are possible from the Black Brook parking area along the coast until you crest the hill beyond Jigging Cove. Near Neils Harbour, on the beach, or on the Jigging Cove trails there is either a weak signal or none at all.

Further Information: David Lawley's book, *A Nature and Hiking Guide to Cape Breton's Cabot Trail*, provides substantial detail on all three trails.

Fishing Cove

Length: 15 km (9.5 mi) return

Time: 6 hr

Type: former road, walking path

Rating(1-5): 4 (distance, steepness)

Uses: hiking, cross-country skiing

Facilities: outhouses, campsites, garbage cans, firewood, benches, fire boxes

Gov't Topo Map: Pleasant Bay 11 K/15

Trailhead GPS Reference: N 46° 45" 40.2' W 60° 50" 04.1'

Access Information: From the Cheticamp park entrance,

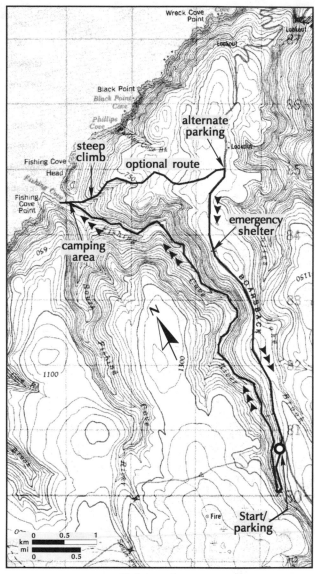

Fishing Cove

drive 22 km (13.75 mi) north along the Cabot Trail, or, from Pleasant Bay, drive 10 km (6.25 mi) south. A road sign indicates the turnoff to the parking lot, which is just off the highway on the ocean side. The trail begins at the far end of the lot.

Introduction: Once the site of a lobster cannery, Fishing Cove was abandoned by the last residents in 1915. The Frasiers, Hinkleys, MacKinnons, and MacRaes who originally settled the deep ravine left for other parts of Cape Breton Island looking for a better life than the precarious existence afforded in their remote refuge. After you have visited Fishing Cove, you may find it difficult to believe people chose to live in such isolation, despite the striking beauty of the surrounding landscape.

Fishing Cove is now the only designated wilderness camping area in the park, with eight tenting sites, and people who stay there once almost always return. Falling asleep to the sound of the surf, swimming in the sheltered cove in either salt or fresh water, and experiencing the remoteness makes this a special place for many who visit. Of all the possible hikes, Fishing Cove was the one most people insisted I include in *Hiking Trails of Cape Breton*. The walk is challenging and the terrain rugged, but the rewards are incomparable. And although it is possible to complete the trail in one day, its difficulty encourages spreading the hike over two days and taking advantage of the camping in the cove area.

From its start on the ridge-line above, the trail loses 335 m (1100 ft) in its descent to the ocean. With several climbs in the middle of the hike, more than 500 m (1640 ft) of uphill walking is required on the round trip. This is not a hike to be attempted casually. I do not recommend it for young children or novice hikers. Always carry extra water and food, and be prepared for changing weather conditions.

Trail Description: The path is initially a continuation of the former route of the main highway, now considerably overgrown. A metal gate prevents vehicles from entering the trail. The pleasant but deceiving aspect of this walk is that the route in is predominantly downhill, and in the first few kilometres the drop is substantial. The old road descends the hillside rather briskly until it reaches Fishing Cove Creek. Spare a moment to examine the old bridge, labelled "unsafe," that spans the ravine. The trail turns sharply right and enters the woods on the narrow footpath. The path follows a wonderful, constricted, steep-sided ravine, hanging onto the slope above the creek like a goat track because there is no room at the bottom of the V-shaped valley for anything but water. At times you are quite high above the cascading stream with nothing to stop you from falling if you are careless. The trail is distinct and well-maintained; small bridges span places where rain water falls down the steep hillside, and numerous benches provide much-needed rest areas for the return climb. The woods are magnificent, but views are scarce because the valley is so narrow and winding, and tree cover in summer and fall is quite thick.

In one or two areas, tough climbing is required on the trip down, and the trail makes several switchbacks at the steepest sections. Fortunately, you will find benches near the top of the worst climbs from either direction, offering a valuable respite. Your first glimpse of the ocean comes at the top of the steepest stretch, and at the bottom of this hill the trail broadens and becomes surfaced with spruce needles as it rejoins the brook. Near the cove, the hills recede, and the final few hundred metres are almost level. Advancing through a spruce thicket, you abruptly emerge onto a large grassy field overlooking a beautiful, tiny inlet and large fresh water pond.

Once there, explore the headlands or just lie on the grass and eat lunch. If you are staying overnight, select

Fishing Cove, the only designated wilderness camping area in Cape Breton Highlands National Park, is popular with hikers and kayakers.

your site and set up camp; firewood is available, brought in by boat and thrown onto the beach. There are out-houses as well. Should you plan on hiking back out the same day, a short rest is in order in any case, and in summer a bracing swim in the cool pond will be very refreshing.

For your return, you may choose to follow a much steeper track which climbs 230 m (750 ft) in less than 1 km (.5 mi), and more than 300 m (1000 ft) in 3 km (1.75 mi). Starting at the spruce thicket near your approach route, this well-defined path follows a tiny brook almost straight up the hill until it connects with the Cabot Trail near the crest of MacKenzies Mountain. Unlike the main trail, however, it offers no benches for rests. At the junction with the highway, turn right and follow the pavement over the Boarsback approximately 5 km (3 mi) to the trailhead. Along the way, there are several viewing stations for drivers that you may wish to use as well. The first of these, on your right, permits you to see Fishing Cove from the road. Along your way, you will also pass one of the park's emergency shelters, situated just off the road on your left.

Cautionary Notes: This rugged trail follows a steep ravine to the ocean. You are often on a narrow track carved into a steep slope, so do not stumble. As there is no secure water source on this hike, be sure to carry an adequate supply.

A backcountry use permit is required for overnight camping. Reserve early in the year to ensure a spot, particularly for long weekends.

If you return on the alternate route and hike alongside the highway for five kilometres, be very cautious of the fast-moving traffic.

Cell Phone Coverage: The only signals strong enough to complete a call throughout the entire route are at the mouth of Fishing Cove Brook and at the top of the Boarsback.

Franey Mountain

Length: 7.5 km (4.75 mi) return

Uses: hiking, cross-country skiing

Time: 3 hr

Facilities: outhouses, garbage cans

Type: walking path, former road, dirt road

Rating (1-5): 3

Gov't Topo Map: Ingonish 11 K/9
Trailhead GPS Reference: N 46° 39" 39.7' W 60° 25" 21.8'

Access Information: From the national park's Ingonish campground, drive 1.5 km (1 mi) north. A large road sign across from the beach at Ingonish Centre directs you

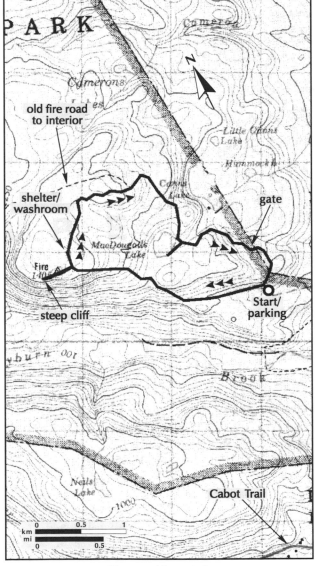

old fire road
to interior

shelter/
washroom

gate

Fire

steep cliff

Start/
parking

Cabot Trail

Franey Mountain

left off the main highway. Follow this road as it changes from pavement to dirt and climbs 1.1 km (.75 mi) to the trailhead. Driving another kilometre takes you to a small parking area in front of a gate that blocks further travel. Those wishing an easier hike may follow the remains of the road from here to the tower and back.

Introduction: The path up Franey Mountain is one of my favourite hikes because it leads to one of the best hilltop views in the province. However, getting there requires uncommon effort; this trail is particularly challenging. Within 2.5 km (1.5 mi) you climb 366 m (1200 ft). Though not unusual elsewhere, such an elevation change is almost unique among Nova Scotia hiking trails and is certain to surprise both the novice and the imprudent. I have rated this trail a 3, requiring some level of fitness to complete, but approaching the fire tower from the direction of the former road is somewhat easier.

Trail Description: I recommend starting at the lower parking area and climbing, rather than descending, the steep section of this trail. This route is easier on muscles and joints, as walking uphill is less wearing than going downhill. If you have knee problems, I suggest parking at the upper lot and both ascending and descending on the former road.

From the lower lot, the trail enters the woods and initially climbs gradually. The approach road has already shaved 120 m (400 ft) from your climb, leaving only about 300 m (1000 ft) remaining to the summit. You also start on a small plateau between steep elevation changes, permitting some warm-up before the tough climbing. The trail is very well constructed and maintained, gravel surfaced at the start with logs set diagonally at intervals to divert runoff. It is also wide enough for two to walk side by side. On your right you see the ridge-line that will be your first objective. It is about 120 m (400 ft) above the start, and there is another small plateau there.

Within a kilometre you reach the first steep section. The trail becomes narrower and rockier and starts to hug the hillside more. As you climb you begin to glimpse the hills on the far side of the Clyburn Valley. They are higher than your location now, but by the end of the hike you will be looking over them. A small viewing spot provides an unobstructed vista up the Clyburn River and also of the fire tower. You get a brief respite just beyond that point, where the trail descends slightly into a little ravine. At the back of the gully a beautifully clear brook bubbles down the hill. Drinking untreated water is not recommended, but I find it hard to resist this inviting fountain.

Just the other side of the brook you begin a very steep climb, where an elaborate series of stairs is constructed into the hill. At least you have a lovely little creek on your right during this ascent. Its gurgling almost masks the groans from you and your travelling companions. Portions of this section are heavily eroded and very rocky, but you should find good traction for your boots, and the stairs are invaluable. As you start along the second set of stairs you should be able to see MacDougalls Lake to your right and below. You will also get a good view of South Bay Ingonish and Cape Smokey.

After an eternity (really not much more than a kilometre), you crest a knoll and sight the fire tower at almost the same elevation as you are. On your right is a small open bog. Search for moose droppings, or even for moose. A steep 30 m (100 ft) remains to be climbed, but the views are wonderful, and the horizon is opening up.

Finally, you are there. Expect higher winds and lower temperatures at the summit. Plan as well to spend quite a bit of time sitting on the cliff, about 50 m/yd from the tower, enjoying the view. It is a fair reward for a de-

Franey Mountain lookoff, 400 m (1300 ft) above the Clyburn
River Valley, with Cape Smokey in the distance.

manding walk. Resist the urge to climb the fire tower. The shelter at the top is locked, as is a small cabin nearby. Outhouses are located next to the cabin. To return to your car, follow the former road down the hill and make a loop out of the trail. This route is slightly longer than the hill slope but far easier. It includes only one short climb about a kilometre from the tower, but otherwise the 4 km (2.5 mi) of this path is all downhill.

At MacDougalls Lake a short side trail takes you to the water's edge. Continuing past this trail, the road descends steeply, a boisterous brook accompanying you on your left. You reach the gate and upper parking lot within another 500 m/yd, and the road curves gently right around the hill, affording further superb views of Ingonish Bay. Much faster than you went up, you arrive at the lower parking lot.

Cautionary Notes: The trail takes you to the top of a 400+ metre (1300+ ft) cliff with no safety barriers.

The climb is a steep, difficult effort, so take it easy and rest often. Wear layers so that you may adjust your clothing as your body temperature rises during the climb and falls at the summit.

My GPS registered over 7 km (4.25 mi) on this hike, more than the 6.5 km (4 mi) suggested in park literature.

Cell Phone Coverage: Through most of the hike, especially at the upper elevation, coverage is quite good. At the parking lots and near MacDougalls Lake, no call can be completed.

Further Information: Parks Canada produces a number of brochures, and the trail is shown on their special topographical map of the entire park. This hike is also mentioned in David Lawley's book, *A Nature and Hiking Guide to Cape Breton's Cabot Trail*.

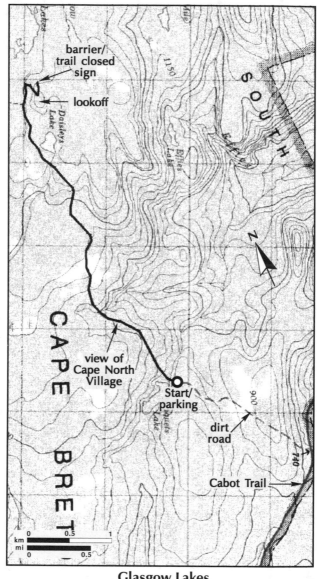

barrier/
trail closed
sign

lookoff

view of
Cape North
Village

Start/
parking

dirt
road

Cabot Trail

km
mi

Glasgow Lakes

Glasgow Lakes

Length: 9.5 km (6 mi)
return
Time: 3 hr
Type: former road,
walking paths
Rating(1-5): 3

Uses: hiking, cross-country
skiing
Facilities: garbage cans

Gov't Topo Map: Dingwall 11 K/16
Trailhead GPS Reference: N 46° 50" 07.1' W 60° 26" 03.0'

Access Information: From Neils Harbour, drive 9 km (5.5 mi) along the Cabot Trail toward Cape North and Dingwall. Road signs indicate the turnoff on the left shortly after the highway begins to descend toward the ocean. A dirt road continues inland for 2 km (1.25 mi), ending at a parking lot by Paquets Lake (Paquette Lake on the park's map).

Introduction: The Glasgow Lakes Trail climbs from 200 m (650 ft) to 440 m (1450 ft) and takes you onto the highlands plateau. Formerly a fire road, the path climbs almost steadily from its start to the windswept barrens of a look-off. From there, views of Cape North Village and Money Point far to the north are possible on clear days.

This is the highest elevation reached by any hike in this book, and environmental conditions here are quite different from almost any other spot in the province. Check with park officials before attempting the hike, especially in April, May, September, or October, and expect it to be cooler and windier near Glasgow Lake than at the start. However, because of its relatively short length and reasonably good track, the Glasgow Lakes Trail offers the best opportunity for most people to experience the highland plateau.

Trail Description: From the parking lot, continue along the former road as it crosses the brook leading from Paquets Lake. The road turns right, away from the lake, and heads uphill toward the highland plateau. Its track is wide and provides comfortable walking for two, although in wet weather — often even in dry weather — many puddles and streams must be sidestepped. Rocks intrude throughout the path, the thin soil here being inadequate to cover the massive granite block constituting the entire highlands.

Quickly the hardwood growing in the sheltered area around Paquets Lake disappears, unable to survive the brutal conditions of the exposed north-facing slope. The fragile-looking larch and balsam fir around you, many barely a metre high, are not new growth but 50 to 75 years old. In winter, high winds drive ice crystals into exposed branches, killing them. Only those parts of the tree covered by snow are able to survive. Like carefully tended shrubs, the new growth is pruned back year after year by the unforgiving climate.

Less than a kilometre from the start, the view north opens up as the trail climbs the slope above Effies Brook. Halfway to Daisleys Lake, the low rise of Mica Hill dominates to your left. The ground in that direction seems open, offering easy walking, but I recommend staying on the path. In addition to the usual safety reasons, the land is sensitive to intrusion, and repeated human use can severely damage it.

Crossing the brook draining from Daisleys Lake may be a challenge. The ground up here is almost always wet, but during or after a rainfall water runs everywhere. The path makes a detour from its original route, now covered by a pond, to connect with a bridge. Even this does not guarantee dry feet, however, so be prepared. Taller trees provide shelter from the wind during the final steep climb toward the lake. As you approach the pond, note that browsing moose have stripped bark from many of the trees to your right. You can reach the water's edge by following one of the many broad trails moose have cleared through the undergrowth.

Beyond Daisleys Lake you encounter several apparent junctions, all unsigned. Wrong turns are possible, and the former trail to Long Lake, on your left and heading downhill, is the most tempting. Continue along the most travelled-looking path, however, and remember that within a kilometre you should find a sign pointing to the look-off on your right. A Trail Closed sign and rope barrier now obstruct further travel along the former road.

Climb the narrow footpath leading over the rocky slope to the knoll. Once on top, you are treated to the view of the Glasgow Lakes and beyond for which you have worked so hard. A Closed sign has also been posted across the path up here to mark the end of the trail. When ready, turn around and retrace your route to the start.

Cautionary Notes: Up on the highland plateau the weather is the most variable and harsh of any in the Maritimes. Always check the latest weather reports before starting, and even then prepare for rain and cold. It is easy to get lost on the barrens, particularly in fog, and it gets foggy often up here.

Park brochures state that this trail is 8 km (5 mi) long, but my GPS registered more than 9 km (5.5 mi), and it usually measures 5-10% short. Be prepared to spend up to an hour longer than you might otherwise expect.

Cell Phone Coverage: At the trailhead and through the first two kilometres, no coverage is available. However, as you enter the barrens and climb toward Daisleys Lake, you should be able to make a connection, except in some low, dead spots near small creeks. At the knoll above the Glasgow Lakes, the coverage is surprisingly good, and it can be quite fun to call someone and describe the view.

Future Plans: Some books and maps show the trail continuing beyond its current endpoint. This former trail has been closed by Parks Canada because of the negative environmental impact of high use, and it is no longer being maintained. Although the trail appears well defined beyond the signs, please venture no further.

Further Information: Parks Canada brochures on trails, flora, and fauna are available. David Lawley's book, *A Nature and Hiking Guide to Cape Breton's Cabot Trail*, also outlines this trail, including the abandoned sections.

MacIntosh Brook

Length: 3 km (1.75 mi) return
Hiking Time: 1 hr
Type of Trail: former cart track, walking path
Rating (1-5): 1

Uses: hiking
Facilities: garbage cans, washrooms, campsites, water, tables, cooking shelter, playground

Gov't Topo Map: Pleasant Bay 11 K/15
Trailhead GPS Reference: N 46° 48" 40.8' W 60° 46" 03.1'

Access Information: From Pleasant Bay, drive east along the Cabot Trail approximately 2.5 km (1.5 mi). The campground is on the right and a warden's cabin on the left of the highway. Turn into the campground; the trail begins at the far end of the parking lot.

Introduction: MacIntosh Brook empties into the Grand Anse River not far from the campsite, and the entire deep

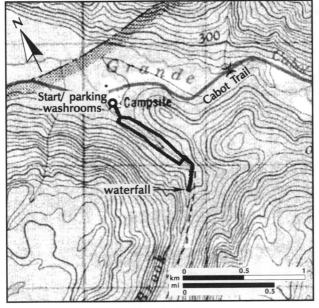

MacIntosh Brook

valley through which the Cabot Trail travels from Pleasant Bay to North Mountain is named for the larger stream. One of the few places in Nova Scotia where the settlers did not clear the original trees, this valley is comprised largely of old sugar maples and may be typical of the pre-settlement Acadian Forest. The Grande Anse Valley has been proposed as an International Biological Programme Reserve, a protected natural area where human influence is kept to a minimum.

Although one of the easiest walks outlined in this book, MacIntosh Brook is worth visiting by everyone. The tall sugar maple trees in the narrow valley provide a storybook forest setting for the walk, and the small waterfall at the end of the trail makes this a pleasant diversion. Wide, dry footpaths provide easy access to almost anyone who wants to complete this enjoyable sylvan stroll.

MacIntosh Brook and Aspy River are the only camping sites in the northern area of the park. The MacIntosh Brook Campground is a natural stop for people spending more than just a weekend in the highlands. In 1998, the local development agency constructed a new shelter complex. Restaurants and gasoline can be found in Pleasant Bay, just 2.5 km (1.5 mi) away, and with running water, flush toilets, sinks, wood stoves, numerous tables, and electricity, there are so many amenities that it is almost embarrassing to admit you have camped here!

Trail Description: A wide gravel path leads from the parking lot to the trailhead, marked by a metal hiking sign. Just past a thin fringe of trees, the former cart track crosses a small field and enters an area of white spruce that is reclaiming former farmlands. MacIntosh Brook can be heard bubbling away on your right, and small side paths lead to the water.

About 200 m/yd from the start, the trail splits, with the right branch crossing the brook. No sign recommends a direction, so continue straight along the old road, now a well-defined pathway, as it moves closer to the ridge line on your left and parallels its steepening slope. Although the path remains fairly level, many roots and rocks, the signs of erosion due to heavy usage, intrude to make walking somewhat tricky. In summer the high canopy of hardwoods provides shelter from the direct light of the sun, and everything appears a lush, vibrant green. In fall, the thick carpet of fallen leaves often conceals the tread-way, sometimes creating short and unplanned detours.

About a kilometre from the trailhead, the two tracks reconnect, the right path recrossing MacIntosh Brook over a sturdy bridge to rejoin the original route. Less than 50 m/yd later, the trail crosses the brook again, moving back over to the west bank. The valley is much narrower here, and rocky outcropppings force the path to veer around them to remain near brook level. The hills rise steeply now on both sides and are quite close together. As a result, your GPS Receiver will probably not be able to register a position.

However, only a short distance remains, and as the path hugs the rock face, the brook turns sharply right, forcing the trail to conform. Suddenly you are at the bottom of the falls, the water cascading down a narrow, deeply etched gorge from the hills above. A small pool, probably not deep enough for a swim, sits at the base of the cataract, the bare rocks surrounding it constituting the slippery final few metres of the route.

On the return, take the left branch at the trail junction by the lower of the two bridges. Rather than remaining near MacIntosh Brook, this excellent footpath wanders among the trees through the widest part of the narrow valley. Take time to look at the plant life. More than 20 species of fern have been identified in this area, and rare arctic-alpine plants, such as green spleenwort, can be found by the knowledgeable. When you notice the hill on your left looming quite close, the path turns right and crosses another well-constructed bridge to rejoin the path on the east bank. Turn left and follow the old cart track back to the campground.

Cautionary Notes: none.

Cell Phone Coverage: No signal could be obtained at any point on this trail.

Further Information: Parks Canada brochures on trails, flora, and fauna are available and helpful on this walk. David Lawley's book, *A Nature and Hiking Guide to Cape Breton's Cabot Trail,* and Allan Billard's *Waterfalls of Nova Scotia* both mention MacIntosh Brook.

Skyline

Length: 7 km (4.25 mi)
return
Time: 2 hr
Type: walking path
Rating (1-5): 2

Uses: hiking, cross-country
skiing
Facilities: outhouses,
garbage cans

Gov't Topo Map: Pleasant Bay 11 K/15, Cheticamp
River 11 K/10
Trailhead GPS Reference: N 46° 44" 37.5' W 60° 52" 49.9'

Access Information: From the park entrance near Cheticamp, drive 15 km (9.25 mi) north on the Cabot Trail.
Near the summit of French Mountain, a sign directs you
left off the pavement onto a gravel road. Continue along
this for 1 km (.5 mi) to a parking lot.

Introduction: Skyline Trail is a 7 km (4.25 mi) loop that
leads to a steep headland cliff overlooking the Gulf of St.
Lawrence. This relatively easy hike along the high plateau
is one of the most popular day hikes in the park. The
trail is well maintained from start to finish, with all the
deadfall speedily removed during the summer season.
Renovations made by Les Amies du Plein Air, a non-profit
society of friends of the national park, have substantially improved both the treadway and drainage of the
path from the parking area to the coast.

Because of this trail's popularity, extensive boardwalks
were built in 1998 near the headland to reduce the
damage to fragile plants from the many walkers and to
protect some of the most vulnerable sites from human
intrusion. Interpretative panels explaining the situation are
located where the trail emerges from the vegetation.
Please respect the warnings and limit your access to the
areas indicated.

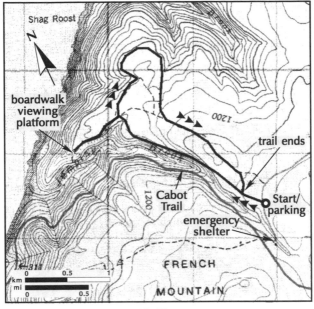

Skyline

Trail Description: The trail begins behind the outhouses at the parking lot and quite gently descends toward the water through ragged patches of tamarack, black spruce, and balsam fir. For the first 500 m/yd both entrance and exit are along the same route, but at a well-signed junction you must choose your approach to the cliffs. The attraction for most people is the point where the long barren spur follows Jumping Brook as it winds toward the ocean. To get there quickest, turn left. For the next 2 km (1.25 mi) your route parallels the ravine on your left, and occasionally you catch glimpses of the sea and French Mountain through the spotty vegetation. There are also a few places where noticeable side trails take you to particularly good viewing locations.

A forest fire ravaged these slopes in 1951, and even

though many of the trees are almost 40 years old, they are only 2.5-3 m (8-10 ft) high. The poor soil and extreme weather conditions combine to prevent healthy growth. Only in sheltered areas do you find more vigorous trees. Notice also the damage done by browsing moose. They will strip the bark as high as they can reach, and this severely scars many trees.

Another junction with a boardwalk, benches, and a new viewing platform mark the location where you once again connect with the loop. Continue straight ahead for now. Just beyond this point the view opens dramatically onto a thrilling sight: the Gulf of St. Lawrence, stretching across the entire horizon. French Mountain, to your left and below, dominates the south, and the deep ravine containing Jumping Brook is directly beneath you. The path, now all boardwalk with frequent viewing platforms, descends steeply down the slope. Note that there are no railings, so as not to interfere with the view from French Mountain.

Before you reach the final spur you come to a sign warning you that it is closed for hiking, so you must stop here. But this is such a fantastic spot that you may wish to linger. On all sides save your approach, steep cliffs fall precipitously. The crumbling, twisted metamorphic rocks are too unstable to permit climbing. Observe how the birds take flight. Perched on the sheer hillsides, they merely open their wings. They have no need to flap, they are instantly airborne. Watch closely; sometimes there are eagles mixed among the gulls. For most people, the visit to this spot is enough, and they return they way they hiked in. But a further 3 km (2 mi) of trail exists, and it provides your best chance of seeing wildlife. As you climb back up from the spur and re-enter the trees, you return to the junction. Turn left, and follow the path as it takes you another kilometre further toward Georges Brook and above Shag Roost.

From this section, before the path turns inland and climbs back to the parking lot, you get a view of the land in the direction of Fishing Cove. On a clear day, you can sit on one of the benches and possibly sight the Magdalen Islands, nearly 100 km (62 mi) to the north-west. At dusk lights from the islands are often seen from this high vantage point. The trail begins to circle inland and rise slowly as you climb back to the top of the highlands. Pay attention, for moose graze in this area. A visiting friend from the United States walked around a patch of krummholz and almost collided with a 450 kg (1000 lb) bull. Needless to say, he found another way past that point. The trail steers back to the first junction you encountered. Keep left, and a walk of 500 m/yd more puts you back at your car.

Cautionary Notes: Much of the trail follows a cliff edge, and some of that is hidden by vegetation. There are no guard rails, so keep children in sight at all times. The winds at the water's edge will be high and cool. Expect temperatures lower than inland; gale force winds are not uncommon, particularly in late fall and winter.

Recent extensive construction at the headland is designed to protect the environment. Please stay on the boardwalk, and do not continue beyond the Trail Closed sign.

Moose are common, and black bear are occasional visitors. Ask park officials for information about recent sightings, and report your own to park staff immediately. Expect to see moose at dawn and dusk.

Cell Phone: Calls can be completed on the ocean-facing slopes and on the trail paralleling Jumping Brook ravine. Only a weak signal can be obtained in the parking area and on the path near Shag Roost.

Further Information: Parks Canada produces a number of brochures, including a hiking trail pamphlet, and the trail is clearly indicated on their special topographical map of the entire park. These can be obtained at the information centres at Cheticamp and Ingonish.

Warren Lake

Length: 6 km (3.75 mi) return

Time: 1.5 hr

Type: walking path, former road

Rating (1-5): 2

Uses: hiking, cross-country skiing

Facilities: outhouse, garbage cans, picnic tables, fireboxes, covered picnic tables

Gov't Topo Map: Ingonish 11 K/9

Trailhead GPS Reference: N 46° 42" 42.3' W 60° 23" 03.6'

Access Information: From the national park's Ingonish Campground, drive 10.5 km (6.5 mi) north, past Broad Cove Campground. Turn left off the main highway, and you will immediately come to a junction on a dirt road. Go straight, and follow this road for 2 km (1.25 mi) to the trailhead. You will pass the trailhead for the Broad Cove Mountain Trail on the way.

Introduction: Warren Lake is a wonderful recreational site. The trail, following the cart track to the former Warren farm site at the western end of the lake, skirts the water's edge through most of its length. Moose are common visitors here, and mice, frogs, and snakes seem to use the path more than people do. This trail is a good choice for almost any level of walker, and it is particularly suited to families.

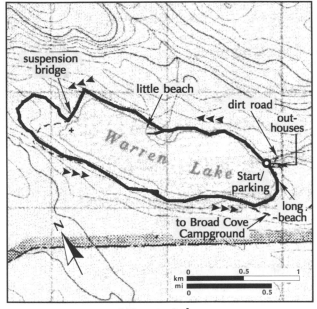

Warren Lake

The eastern end of Warren Lake boasts a long beach composed of a thick sand deposit left behind by the last glacier. It makes an ideal spot for swimming at the end of your walk or a place to enjoy lunch. Hills surround the lake on every side, with Broad Cove Mountain and its short hiking trail dominating the northeast.

The Warren Lake Trail can be accessed directly by car, or by a 2 km (1.25 mi) footpath from the Broad Cove Campground on the coast. The campground is open only during the summer months.

Trail Description: The path starts near the lakeshore, at the west end of the parking lot, and, comfortably wide for two, it is clearly a former cart-track. Warren Lake is to your left, visible through the hardwoods whose branches shade you from the summer sun. The slope of Broad Cove Mountain climbs, not too steeply, on your right.

For the first few hundred meters the surface is gravelled, although the gravel ends after you cross the first major bridge. From here, grass, earth, and wood chips make up the treadway. The route stays very close to the water for the first kilometre, giving good views up and across the lake. A small knoll compels a minor detour, moving the trail away from the water and requiring you to make a slight climb. You soon return to the lake, but first you cross a sturdy bridge over the small brook that empties the waters of Cradle Lake, high above. It's a mere trickle in the summer, but its ravaged banks hint at its powerful flow during the spring run-off.

Near the mouth of the brook, just past the headland, you will find a tiny beach with a bench beside it. The trail continues past the beach, following the shore until it begins to climb the steepening slope at the northwest corner of the lake. Turning left, the path descends into an area of white spruce, where a bridge crosses a small stream. You are near the halfway point now, and when you reach a little field, site of the former farm, you have reached the banks of Warren Brook, where a wonderful suspension bridge transports you to the far side.

Once across, you enter mature hardwood on a grassy treadway, passing under towering sugar maples and beech, some of them over 2 m (6-7 ft) in circumference. Moving upstream initially, the path gradually curves left through almost 180° to face back in the direction of the start and climbs more than 15 m (50 ft) above lake level to follow a lovely hardwood slope. It narrows as well, from a cart track to a one-person footpath.

The slope is much steeper on this side of the lake, and wet spots become extremely frequent. Bridges cross narrow but deep ravines cut into the hillside, and small boardwalks can be found almost every 100 m/yd. Considerable effort has been made to provide adequate ditching and drainage for the trail. However, so much precipitation falls in the highlands, and so little is retained by the shallow soil, that you are certain to end up with wet feet, even in fairly dry weather.

Descending almost to water level, the trail follows the shore, with regular bridges and boardwalks. By the time you reach a new boardwalk with a bench on it, you have passed the worst of the wet spots. In the final kilometre, the trail begins to widen and gravel appears once again on the treadway. There is even sand filling some wet spots. The trees here are very young, pin-cherry and striped maple growing among many dead spruce.

You encounter one final boardwalk, nearly at the eastern end of the lake, just before you reach the junction with the path to the Broad Cove Campground. Turn right to walk to the campground, nearly 2 km (1.25 mi) away, 4 km (2.5 mi) return. To get back to your car, turn left, and follow the trail as it stays inside the trees immediately behind the long, sandy beach at this end of Warren Lake. You might stop at one of the picnic tables there and have lunch. At the far end, you must cross a large bridge over Warren Brook to get to the parking lot on the other side and finish your hike.

Cautionary Notes: This is a popular grazing area for moose, especially at dawn and dusk. In their rutting season, the late fall, males can get very aggressive. Do not approach them too closely.

Cell Phone Coverage: There is no cell phone coverage anywhere on this trail.

Future Plans: The park plans continued improvement of the treadway, including more gravel on wet areas.

Further Information: Parks Canada produces a number of brochures, and the trail is shown on their special topographical map of the entire park. This hike is also mentioned in David Lawley's book, *A Nature and Hiking Guide to Cape Breton's Cabot Trail*.

CAPE BRETON HIGHLANDS

Although Cape Breton Highlands National Park is set in the Cape Breton Highlands, it occupies less than half of the land area of this geographical region. Most of the northern parts of Inverness and Victoria counties are comprised of this distinct landscape with its impressive scenery. As you might expect, the Highlands offer numerous hiking opportunities. Indeed, some of the most superb backpacking in Nova Scotia can be found north of the national park. I have profiled five walks in this relatively small area, as well as five others in the much larger area south of the park.

The Cape Breton Highlands is unlike any other part of the province or any other part of Cape Breton Island. It contains the oldest rocks in the region, about 1.2 billion years old. Numerous fault lines have defined the steep sides of its hills and influenced the drainage patterns of many streams. The region's weather is the harshest in the province, noted for its long, cold winters and short, cool summers. More precipitation, approximately 1600 mm (63 in), falls here than anywhere else in Nova Scotia, and its annual snowfall, usually in the range of 400 cm (13 ft), covers the ground until late April or early May.

Most of the communities in the Highlands are along the coastline, and very few roads penetrate the interior hills. Although the original European settlers in the early 1800s, many of whom were Scottish, attempted to raise crops or sheep, most soils are marginal, and the farms have almost all been abandoned. Many residents depend upon the sea for their livelihood, although tourism is an important seasonal employer.

Many of the trails I selected in the Highlands are more difficult than those in other parts of the Island, although the Cabots Landing Provincial Park, Usige Ban Falls, and White Point trails are suitable for almost anyone. Due to the rougher terrain and greater elevation change, Tenerife Mountain is one that I strongly recommend be approached with caution. Portree – Big Intervale, in the Margaree Valley, is almost completely overgrown by brush, but it is almost impossible to get lost as long as you stay at river level. The North River Provincial Park Trail delivers you to the foot of the highest waterfall in Nova Scotia, but you should be prepared to spend most of the day on the return trip. Money Point, requiring two steep climbs, will challenge anyone who undertakes it.

Hunting is permitted in the areas of the Englishtown, Meat Cove, Money Point, Portree – Big Intervale, and Tenerife Mountain trails. Hunting season usually starts around the first of October, but the date varies from year to year and according to species. Contact the Department of Natural Resources for detailed information before going into the woods. Although hunting is not permitted on Sundays, wear bright orange every day in season for safety's sake.

Hikers familiar with the spectacular Polletts Cove Trail will note its absence from *Hiking Trails of Cape Breton*. Although surrounded by thousands of hectares of crown land, approximately 162 h (400 a) of the land at the mouth of the cove to which the hiking path leads is privately owned, and the landowner denied permission to describe the trail in this book.

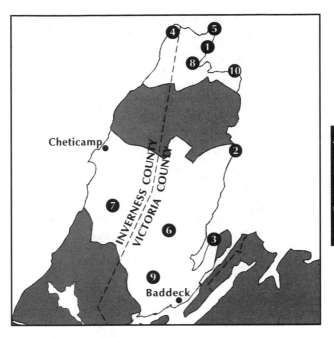

CAPE BRETON HIGHLANDS

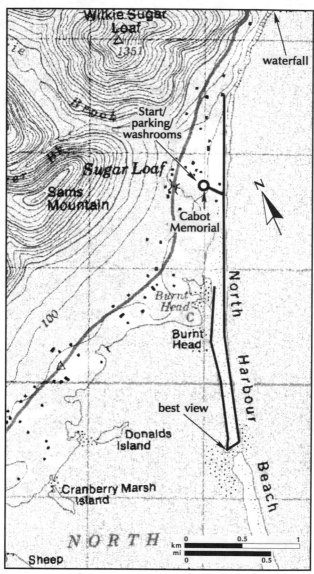

Wilkie Sugar Loaf
△
1351

waterfall

Brook

Start/
parking/
washrooms

Sugar Loaf

Sams
Mountain

Cabot
Memorial

N

Burnt
Head
C

100

Burnt
Head

North Harbour Beach

best view

Donalds
Island

Cranberry Marsh
Island

NORTH

Sheep

| km | 0 | 0.5 | 1 |
| mi | 0 | 0.5 | |

Cabots Landing Provincial Park

Cabots Landing Provincial Park

Length: 6-7 km (3.75-4.25 mi) return
time: 2 hr
Type: beach
Rating (1-5): 1

Uses: hiking, beach recreation
Facilities: garbage cans, picnic tables, barbecue pits

Gov't Topo Map: Dingwall 11 K/16
Trailhead GPS Reference: N 46° 56" 32.3' W 60° 27" 46.7'

Access Information: From Cape North, turn off the Cabot Trail heading toward Bay St. Lawrence and Meat Cove. Follow signs to the park turnoff on the right, approximately 10 km (6.25 mi). Drive to the parking area at the water's edge. Begin your walk southward along the beach.

Introduction: Nova Scotia has more than 400 beaches, all quite lovely. North Harbour Beach, however, enjoys a setting unlike any other I know in this province. It is bordered on three sides by the mountains of the Cape Breton Highlands. South and west lies the plateau of the National Park, rising toward the highest point in the province, White Hill (538 m – 1765 ft), while across the northern skyline runs the Aspy Fault, climbing almost 400 m (1300 ft) within two kilometres of the provincial park entrance. The beach is almost in the middle of a V of mountains, with the open mouth being Aspy Bay and Cabot Strait.

Even without the mountains, the beach is exceptionally attractive, lying at the mouth of North Harbour, or North Pond, which is several kilometres long and drains the North Aspy River into the ocean. The beach extends from near the community of Sugar Loaf in a gentle arc, equal portions sparkling sand and verdant grasses, and aims directly toward the often fog-shrouded heights of

South Mountain. It has a break to permit the waters of North Pond to escape, but you can walk for more than 2.5 km (1.5 mi) south from the parking lot.

Bird life here is quite varied. Inside North Pond lie several large sandy islands heavily populated with arctic terns. They are in the air constantly, patrolling the swiftly moving waters where the pond empties into Aspy Bay. They share these islands with several species of gull and with the ever-present bald eagles perched in trees nearby. The view from the outflow of North Pond is worth the walk: the swiftly moving water, the terns hovering and diving, the rippling outflow extending far out into the bay, and the mountains cradling the Aspy Valley.

For a surprise when you are in the parking area, look at the large hill, Wilkie Sugar Loaf, to the west. About halfway up you will see little white specks. Through binoculars, you will find that someone has painted several mountain sheep on a high, sheer rock face!

Trail Description: This is one of the very few trails where you can see almost the entire route from the start. North Harbour Beach stretches to your right in a broad arc. Leave the Cabot Memorial, cross the lawn by the parking lot, and descend the gentle earthen bank to the soft sand. On this trail, unlike most, where sturdy footwear is essential, you might even consider removing your shoes and completing the walk barefoot.

Beachcombing, birdwatching, and binocular use are recommended for the next two hours. You will seldom enjoy as much horizon in Nova Scotia as you will from the end of this beach. The hills, while they surround the Aspy Valley, are several kilometres away, so you benefit from an almost unlimited view in every direction. When you reach the outflow of North Pond, you may decide to follow the shoreline as it continues behind the beach along the pond. I found the ripple pattern in the sand, created by the rapid flow of the river near the outflow, extremely interesting. Watch out for the jellyfish left behind at low tide, especially if you decided to hike in bare feet!

The sights and sounds of the pond are quite different from those you experience when you're facing the ocean. The water is much calmer, and numerous ducks and small shorebirds shelter from the waves on the more dynamic pond side. Eventually the beach ends in trees and swamp. You may notice paths through the beach grasses, but I recommend that you retrace your route along the water's edge. There is no need to disturb the delicate vegetation of the dunes.

The beach also extends north as if heading towards the mountains and Cape North. Unlike the southern section of the beach, which is quite exposed, the northern section is bounded by a cliff, which increases in height as you approach the long, elevated ridge line known as North Mountain. As you walk, the beach becomes narrower and the cliff gets higher. You can continue to walk for more than 1 km (.5 mi), until you literally run into the wall of North Mountain. The soft reddish tills of the Aspy Valley give way to the grey, more erosion-resistant talus of Money Point and Cape North; from here north, the cliff rises vertically out of the ocean. From the far northern end of the beach, you can observe Pollys Brook empty into the ocean as a waterfall near an outcropping known as Halibut Head. This is a favourite location for sea kayakers.

Cautionary Notes: The beach is quite exposed to wind and waves, and during storms the water can break over the entire width of the dunes. If you are uncertain about conditions, ask local residents and heed their advice.

On summer days make certain you are wearing a hat and sunscreen. There is no shade anywhere on this walk.

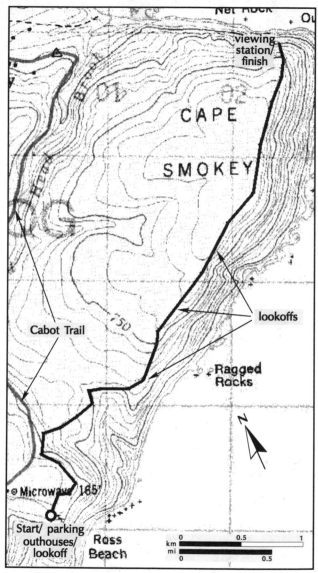

Cape Smokey Provincial Park

Cell Phone Coverage: I could obtain no signal anywhere along the beach, except for a slight flicker at the far north end. Do not expect your phone to work.

Further Information: Near the parking lot is a large display area commemorating the possible landing of Sir John Cabot near this spot in 1497. There is also a plaque detailing the landing of the first trans-Atlantic communication cable in this area in the late 19th century.

Cape Smokey Provincial Park

Length: 11 km (6.75 mi) return
Time: 3-4 hr
Type: walking paths
Rating (1-5): 3

Uses: hiking, cross-country skiing
Facilities: outhouses, picnic tables, garbage cans

Gov't Topo Map: Ingonish 11 K/9
Trailhead GPS Reference: N 46° 35" 36.2' W 60° 22" 50.0'

Access Information: On the Cabot Trail and at the top of perhaps the most famous hill on Cape Breton Island, this hike can be found easily by anybody. But, if a place-name helps, it is 13 km (8 mi) south from Ingonish Beach and the entrance to the Cape Breton Highlands National Park. A large sign at the highest point of the road directs you into the picnic park toward the shoreline. The trail starts at the north side of the parking lot.

Introduction: Most people's memory of the Cabot Trail includes Smokey Mountain. Perhaps it is the unbelievably steep climb to the summit, or maybe it is the awesome panorama of the Atlantic Ocean spreading out beyond and below as you ascend, or possibly it is the spectacular view of the lowlands of Wreck Cove, Birch Plain, and Skir Dhu stretching south until lost in the mists. Whatever the reason, this place has a magical effect on people's imaginations.

The park is opposite the road's highest point and on the edge of the shoreline cliff. Communities of industrial Cape Breton, Glace Bay, New Waterford, and Sydney Mines are visible on clear days, despite being more than 50 km (31 mi) distant, and the massive smokestacks of the coal-fired electric generator at Point Aconi are unmistakable. At night the lights to the south pattern a vast arc which seems to appear out of the water.

Picnic tables and washrooms are located beside the parking lot, and many people hike no further than the nearest empty bench. After all, the magnificent view is the big attraction. But if you want an interesting hike and the chance for a different vista, move toward the trail-head.

Trail Description: The first 500 m/yd of the path are wide, open, and gravelled. Fires devastated most of the park in the 1940s, and the poor soil and exposed location have made regrowth slow and patchy. At the beginning of the hike only a few scrawny birch and cherry trees break the wind. As the trail curves left back toward the highway, the shelter created by the hill permits healthier growth.

Virtually the only wet areas of the hike are found in the first kilometre, and none of these areas is particularly bad. The granite rocks here date from the late Ordovician period, 450 million years ago, and, although traces of sandstone overlay remain on the north-side incline, most has long since eroded away. As in most granite districts, especially those with frequent high winds, only a thin layer of soil has gathered in hollows and protected spots, resulting in limited vegetation and poor drainage.

Turning away from the road, the trail descends rapidly into a fairly open barren. An area of richer soil at the lowest elevation contains white spruce and balsam fir, and there is a bench beside the small bridge over a brook.

Climbing out of the sheltered ground, you come to a lookoff on your right, at the cliff edge above open terrain. There are several similar stations along the ridge top, all with comparable views and most with benches. Climbing 105 m (350 ft) over the next 1.5 km (1mi), the trail continues through areas once devastated by fire. Because of the scarcity of tall trees, many of the red rectangular markers designating the path are mounted at the top of stakes positioned beside the trail. Yellow markers affixed on the other side indicate the return route.

You climb over the top of Cape Smokey, more than 30 m (100 ft) higher than the parking area. Expect to find fresh moose scat (if not a fresh moose!) everywhere, and notice how the browsing of moose has damaged many of the trees. Look for evidence of bobcat and coyote, as well as their dinner, snowshoe hare. The vegetation along the top is far more rugged than on the protected slopes.

The final kilometre of the trail descends about 90 m (300 ft) to a lookoff on South Bay Ingonish. You are near the headland of Cape Smokey, as the sound of the buoy off Stanley Point indicates. The trees here, some of the few survivors of the fire, are far healthier than any others you have seen on this hike. A 200-year-old yellow birch helps you visualize what the original forest of birch, spruce, and fir must have looked like.

Your view is north and west toward new sights. Keltic Lodge, one of Nova Scotia's most famous resorts, gleams white against the greens of Middle Head, the thin peninsula bisecting the huge bay. Ingonish Beach, more than 2 km (1.25 mi) long, draws a golden line to your left dividing land and sea. You should be able to spot the fire tower on top of Franey Mountain, another essential hiking destination described in *Hiking Trails of Cape Breton*. Stay

On the Cape Smokey Trail, don't be surprised to see moose.

behind the barrier because it is situated just above a 180-m (600-ft) cliff. Lean on the railing, take a few photographs, and prepare for the hike back. This is a linear trail, so you must return the way you hiked in.

Cautionary Notes: Some of the viewing points are at the top of a 275-m (900-ft) cliff. Remain behind the barriers. Do not venture along the ridge line at the south end of the park, despite the appearance of paths. This is not part of the trail system, and the footing is very uncertain.

There is no water available on the trail; carry your own.

Weather conditions on the exposed cape are often extreme. The French name, Cape Enfumé, was given because of the clouds that always seem to cling to these slopes. Expect high winds often, and be prepared for rapid weather changes.

Cell Phone Coverage: Strong coverage throughout the entire hike.

Further Information: A brochure, *Provincial Hiking Trails of Victoria County*, can be obtained by contacting the Nova Scotia Department of Natural Resources.

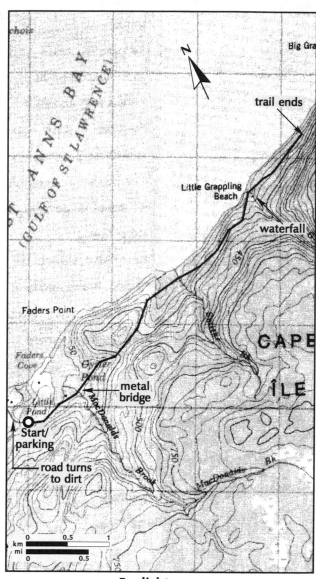

Englishtown

Englishtown

Length: 10 km (6.25 mi) return

Time: 3 hr

Type: dirt road

Rating (1-5): 3

Uses: hiking, biking, horseback riding, ATVs

Facilities: none

Gov't Topo Map: Bras d'Or 11 K/8
Trailhead GPS Reference: N 46° 17" 46.2" W 60° 31" 13.8'

Access Information: About 22 km (14 mi) east of Baddeck on Highway 105, take Exit 12 onto Route 312. Turn left toward the Englishtown ferry and Ingonish. Continue straight past the Englishtown ferry at 6 km (3.75 mi); the pavement runs out after 2 km (1.25 mi). Continue along the dirt road for another 500 m/yd as it descends to cross Sallys Brook. Just past there, the road forks. Park and start walking the right-hand route.

Introduction: Situated opposite the long sandy beach separating St. Anns Harbour from the Gulf of St. Lawrence, Englishtown has enjoyed an extensive history of settlement. The Denys brothers established a farming and trading post at what they called Ste. Anne in the early 1700s, and when the French were considering where to establish their major fortress on Ile Royale, it was very nearly placed here instead of at Louisbourg. The community earned its present name in about 1820, when it was called Bhal na Ghul, or "Town of the English," because the settlers who arrived in the 1780s could not speak Gaelic.

In the late 1980s, plans to mine gypsum from Cape Dauphin Mountain led to the extension of the former road beyond Englishtown far up the coastline. However, public opposition to the proposed quarry cancelled further development, and the mine was never built. Now the road intended for large trucks has mostly grown over with alders, but it is still relatively easy walking, with excellent bridges crossing the turbulent brooks that foam down the slopes of Kellys Mountain.

Trail Description: Your track is the remains of the old road, so it is wide and open for most of the hike. From the start, you climb a short distance, then gently descend the remaining 600 m/yd to MacDonalds Brook. Oyster Pond is visible to your left through the trees, while the slope of Kellys Mountain climbs nearby on your right. At the brook, which is a little wider than you can leap across, you will find an odd-looking metal bridge with no railings. It is safe for walking, and ATVs probably use it.

Once across MacDonalds Brook, the trail starts to climb relatively steeply, probably the toughest part of the hike. Logging on both sides opens up the view considerably, and you can gain good views of Oyster Pond and Murray Mountain across St. Anns Bay. The footing also gets rougher as you climb, with deep gouges having been cut in the treadway by runoff.

The climb continues for more than 800 m/yd, and a knoll rises on your left as you approach the highest point of the walk, restricting further views of the ocean. Descending again, the treadway becomes quite grassy. A small brook on your right parallels your course until you reach the bottom again, where it passes underneath the road. Shortly before this point, a small track branches left into the forest and leads about 300 m/yd from the main trail to the remains of a house, now nearly hidden in the vegetation. Once past this junction, the road changes substantially, becoming wider and less rutted and having a sandier surface.

A further 200 m/yd brings you to the well-constructed bridge crossing Smiths Brook, 3 km (1.75 mi) from the start. You are still too far inland to see the ocean, so continue to follow the road as it climbs again on the far side of the brook. This time the ascent is more gradual and not nearly as challenging. Unlike the earlier portions of the trail, however, alders have grown along the sides of the path, and in the summer they nearly obscure it. Even when the leaves have fallen, their branches are high enough to be annoying, and mountain bikers will definitely suffer. For most of the next kilometre you must pick your way through the young, thick growth. The treadway remains distinct, however, and you also regain your view of St. Anns Bay and the hills of the Highlands on the far side.

After a last short climb, the trail bends left toward the ocean, and you will recognize Cape Smokey far up the coast. You begin to descend quite briskly now, and a few minor detours are required to avoid some larger birch which have fallen across the path, the first substantial blockages. Stop at the bottom of the hill when you reach the massive bridge over the deep, narrow gorge of Grappling Brook. You have several options at this point. Just before the bridge, a distinct footpath on the left leads you an easy 20 m/yd to the coastline and the pink granite of Little Grappling Beach, a wonderful spot to sit and enjoy a snack. About 50 m/yd upstream, after a difficult scramble over the rocks, you will find a marvellous pool of cold, clear mountain water fed from a tiny waterfall. A perfect fit for a couple, it is surrounded on all sides by steep rock faces and thick vegetation. Be careful, because footing is difficult, and the pool cannot be seen from the trail.

Beyond Grappling Brook, almost one kilometre of trail remains. Climbing again, the former road follows the coastline, and you get good views of rocky hillsides as Cape Dauphin Mountain veers to cross your path. During this part of the hike, you cross from the Victoria Coastal Plain natural region to the steep slope of the Cape Breton Highlands.

Suddenly the path simply ends, with a small creek cutting across the road. The ocean is quite near on your left, but the coastline here is a cliff, so be cautious. No further trail continues toward Big Grappling Beach, and the slope of the hillside beyond this point becomes too steep for most people. Instead, stop here, then retrace your route back to the start.

Cautionary Notes: Hunting is permitted on these lands.

Cell Phone Coverage: At lower elevations on the trail, only a weak signal can be obtained and no call completed. On the hilltops and on many of the slopes, a call can be made. No connection is possible at either trailhead or endpoint of the hike. Calling is possible from Little Grappling Beach.

Meat Cove

Length: 16 km (10 mi)
return
Time: 6 hr
Type: former roads,
animal trails
Rating (1-5): 4 (distance,
steepness)

Uses: hiking, mountain
biking, cross-country
skiing, ATVs,
snowmobiling
Facilities: camping, tables,
water, outhouses

Gov't Topo Map: Cape St. Lawrence 11 N/2
Trailhead GPS Reference: N 47° 01" 34.4' W 60° 33" 32.6'

Access Information: From Cape North Village, turn off the Cabot Trail onto an unnumbered road toward Bay St. Lawrence. After driving north 14 km (8.75 mi), look for the turnoff to Capstick and Meat Cove on the left. For the first 6 km (3.75 mi) the road is paved, but the last 7 km (4.25 mi) is a narrow dirt road. Follow it until it ends at the McLellan's Meat Cove Campground, where the trail begins. Parking is available, with a $2 charge.

Introduction: This is the trail at the end of the earth, or so you may think as you drive toward it. The sheer cliffs hugged by the narrow dirt track seem invulnerable to human habitation, and Meat Cove, when you finally see it, appears hopelessly fragile, dwarfed by the rugged hills surrounding it. Meat Cove earned its name in the late 1700s, when the stench of slaughtered moose caused complaints from passing ships.

These hills are an amazingly fertile area for orchids, some found nowhere else in the province; no one seems to know why, exactly. Flower-lovers flock here regularly to find unique plants.

There are several hiking options available, and I am describing only the one found in the original *Walk Cape*

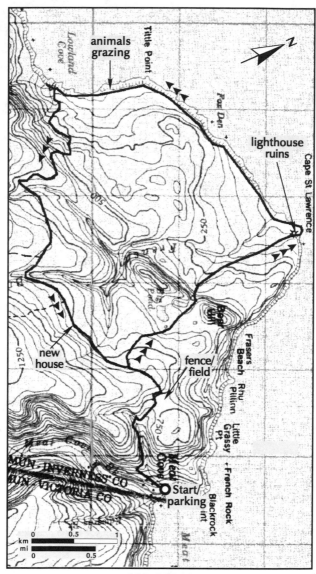

animals grazing

Tittle Point

Fox Den

lighthouse ruins

Cape St. Lawrence

Lowland Cove

new house

fence/ field

Fraser's Beach

Rhu Pillira

Little Grassy Pt.

French Rock

Blackrock Point

Meat Cove

Start/ parking

MUN. INVERNESS CO.
MUN. VICTORIA CO.

Meat

km 0   0.5   1
mi 0   0.5

Meat Cove

Breton book published in 1975. This can be a challenging one-day loop or a more relaxed two-day camp-out. Considering the splendour of Lowland Cove, I recommend spending the extra day. I know few more beautiful places to camp anywhere.

Trail Description: Start uphill along a continuation of the dirt road behind the campground's picnic site. Expect a challenging climb as the road switches back and forth up the hillside. A gate 500 m/yd along restricts vehicular traffic but not hikers. The unmarked and overgrown Old Fraser Road joins on the left at a sharp corner, and after nearly a kilometre, a fence on your right provides a place to lean and rest. The trail continues to climb, turning sharply left just at the gate. Shortly afterward it levels, then starts downhill. Look for an old road forking to the right. This is the junction with the Lighthouse Trail, and flagging tape and yellow metal markers may sign this branch. Follow it.

For the first time larger trees provide cover overhead. While there is still room for two to walk side-by-side, the woods crowd this path more closely. Watch for and follow the yellow markers as you pass numerous side-paths on your gradual descent. After a kilometre, just after passing a small pond on your left, the trail cuts left sharply and plunges down the exceptionally steep and rocky slope of Bear Hill. Mountain bikers should check their brakes before this point! For the final kilometre the descent is gentler, and the trees suddenly end, revealing the grassy coastline of Cape St. Lawrence. The tip of the point is littered with ruins of former lighthouses, and only a small, automated signal remains today. To the right, on a clear day, you can see St. Paul Island, the northernmost place in Nova Scotia.

The trail continues left along the open shoreline. There are no markers here, but the area has long been used as a free range for cattle, and their path along the coast becomes yours. The small, deep gully cut by French Brook is a popular camping site, providing shelter from the restless winds. Continue past it and the Fox Den, a rocky, cliff-lined gorge. Watch for minke whales and pilot whales, common off this coast.

As you round Tittle Point, the breathtaking beauty of Lowland Cove gradually reveals itself. Forested hills enclose the grassy fields in a sheltered bowl that is ideal for camping. Look for horses and cows grazing on the tough grasses clinging to the gentle slopes. The best location for an overnight is at the far end of the cove, close by a small hollow near Lowland Brook, which is also the end of the trail. You can return the way you walked in, thus ensuring the maximum amount of coastal hiking, or you can follow a different route over the hillside behind the open ground of the cove, a route occasionally marked by red rectangular metal signs. Either choice involves steep climbs, although the inland trail does spread them out over a greater distance.

If you choose the inland route, your path will take you over two unbridged but not deep streams. Just past the second, you pass a new house. The owner is doing a great deal of work on both sides of the road, so be prepared for unexpected side-trails. Continue straight, heading uphill, and after about a kilometre you return to the intersection with the Lighthouse Trail, completing the loop. Only 2 km (1.25 mi) remains, and only 300 m/yd is uphill. Trekking downhill into Meat Cove reveals more spectacular views of cliffs and ocean, and the end to a hike you will not soon forget.

Cautionary Notes: Very little signage has been installed, and junctions are not well marked. Definitely carry the topographical map for the area. This is isolated territory, and accurate navigation is essential.

Horses graze on the tough grasses clinging to the gentle slopes of Lowland Cove

Hunting is carried on in these lands. Poaching occurs throughout the year.

At present the Meat Cove – Polletts Cove – Pleasant Bay trail is extremely difficult to follow due to the bogs between Meat Cove and Polletts Cove, and it can only completed by advanced navigators and backpackers.

Cell Phone Coverage: No signal is available at any point.

Future Plans: 27,566 ha (68,115 a) north of Cape Breton Highlands National Park, including much of the land over which you hiked, was designated a protected area by the Nova Scotia Department of Natural Resources in the Wilderness Area Protection Act. Over the next several years DNR hopes to develop a management policy in consultation with local residents.

Further Information: A brochure showing the hiking trails in the Cape North area is available at McLellan's Campground and other local tourist information centres.

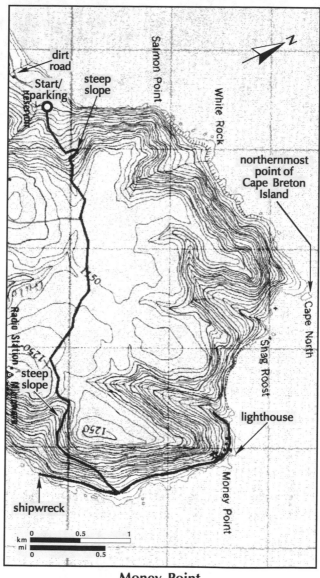

Money Point

Money Point

Length: 16 km (10 mi) return
time: 5-7 hr
Type: beach, ATV trails, rocky cobble
Rating (1-5): 4 (distance, steepness)

Uses: hiking, biking, ATVs, snowmobiling, cross-country skiing
Facilities: none

Gov't Topo Map: Cape North 11 N/1
Trailhead GPS Reference: N 47° 00" 47.9' W 60° 26" 21.3'

Access Information: Turn off the Cabot Trail at Cape North Village by Morrison's Restaurant onto the un-numbered road to Bay St. Lawrence and Meat Cove. At 15.5 km (9.75 mi), continue straight past the turnoff to Meat Cove and past the Central Co-op. At the sign for the Motel Sunset Oasis, about 1.8 km (1 mi) further on, turn right. The pavement ends, and the road continues 2.5 km (1.5 mi) to a parking area at the base of the hill just past the last house on the left.

Introduction: At almost the extreme northern tip of Cape Breton Island, Money Point has become the final resting place of many ships lost in the wild storms of the North Atlantic. It received its name after a sailing vessel carrying the pay for the garrison in Quebec was lost nearby. Since then, gold and silver coins have been found in the surrounding sand and rocks.

Money Point is another hike I discovered through the 1975 guide, *Walk Cape Breton*, which describes it as "mountainous, coastal." After completing it myself, I can recommend it to anyone with mountain goat in his or her ancestry. Requiring more than 750 m (2500 ft) of vertical climb, this trail demands a certain level of fitness to undertake. I do not recommend it for young children or novices.

Trail Description: The trail is the continuation of the road and begins climbing very steeply immediately. Perhaps ATVs and four-wheel-drive vehicles could struggle further, but regular cars cannot. Within 500 m/yd the treadway has becomes grass, and a look behind reveals Bay St. Lawrence, already far below. A power line crosses overhead, and the trail cuts left to more easily scale the slope. The view on your left through the hardwood is magnificent. In barely 1 km (.5 mi), you have climbed almost 240 m (800 ft), and the entire top of the island, all the way to Meat Cove and Cape St. Lawrence, is spread out beneath you in a vivid tableau. You probably need to rest anyway, so spend a few minutes enjoying this magnificent sight.

Switching back and forth, the track alternates between grass and rugged, rocky cobble. Shortly before reaching the plateau, the slope begins to lessen, a feature typical of Cape Breton's rounded hills. On your right you will notice several microwave towers at a slightly higher elevation, and the power line that crossed the road below rejoins the path. Descending ever so slightly, the trail meets a wide road 1.5 km (1 mi) from the start. Turn left, and follow it over nearly level ground for 1.5 km (1 mi) to the next road junction.

At that junction, follow the road paralleling the power poles as it turns left and begins to descend. The path narrows somewhat, bounded closely by dense alders and beech. Within 200 m/yd, the bottom falls out of the road as it plunges into a narrow ravine. A small clearing on your right, obviously used by cars to turn around, provides a good view of Cabot Strait and Aspy Bay. For the next kilometre your knees will protest as the trail drops down the steep slope, then suddenly you emerge onto an incredibly beautiful narrow coastal plain.

In summer the plain is a riot of flowers and high grasses, constantly buffeted by restless winds. St. Paul Island, the desolate northern outpost of Nova Scotia, 14 km (8.5 mi) beyond Money Point, should be visible on a clear day. Continue following the track and the power poles left, as they head north along the coast. Foundations of abandoned homesteads can be found in the deep grasses, the stone rectangles all that remain of some settler's dreams. As you walk along this shore, watch the ocean. Pilot, fin, and minke whales are common visitors to these waters, and a wide variety of seabirds dot the shoreline and ocean. Kestrels perch on the power wires, wobbling in the breeze, and use the powerful winds to soar effortlessly over the grasslands.

Topping a slight rise, you notice the lighthouse for the first time, its cheery red and white in dramatic contrast to your isolation. Turn left and look up the hillside; it climbs almost vertically for 365 m (1200 ft), and the clouds often appear to be barely scraping over its peak. The grassy road continues until you reach the lighthouse, passing the fragmented remains of wharves in the tiny cove beneath it.

The lighthouse is currently undergoing renovations which will include a new staircase, and the hillside on which it sits is being reinforced. The other buildings, once part of a larger complex, are all gone, leaving nothing but concrete foundations. Access to the lighthouse is restricted; please do no damage to this important structure. Beyond the buildings another field beckons, but only for a further 200 m/yd. When you reach the bushes beside a small creek, stop there, and begin your return hike. This field is an excellent place to camp or just to sit and enjoy lunch.

As an interesting side excursion, continue south along the coastline for about 500 m/yd beyond the turnoff to climb the hill to return. You will find the rusted remains of a small boat scattered along the shore, much of it still intact. At low tide you can walk amongst the wreckage.

Cautionary Notes: Exposed coastline at Money Point and higher elevations often experiences more changeable weather and higher winds than Bay St. Lawrence. Expect unforecast showers and cooler temperatures, even in summer.

This area is very isolated; inform friends of your destination and expected return time.

Hunting is permitted in these hills, and poaching of moose occurs throughout the year.

Cell Phone Coverage: There is no signal at all from Bay St. Lawrence to the plateau area. From there, a weak signal may permit more powerful phones to complete a call. Coming down the hillside facing the Cabot Strait, the signal is at its strongest, weakening again at water level and disappearing when you round Money Point.

Further Information: A brochure showing possible hiking trails in the Cape North area is produced by Meat Cove Camping. Detail about this entire coastline is available in Scott Cunningham's *Sea Kayaking in Nova Scotia*, and Kermit De Gooyer describes this trail in *Mountain Bike Nova Scotia*.

North River Provincial Park

Length: 18 km (11.25 mi) return

Time: 5-7 hr

Type: former road, walking paths, steep slopes

Rating (1-5): 5 (distance, rugged terrain)

Uses: hiking, cross-country skiing

Facilities: outhouses, water, garbage cans, picnic tables, benches

Gov't Topo Map: St. Anns Harbour 11 K/7

Trailhead GPS Reference: N 46° 19" 05.8', W 60° 39" 43.6'

Access Information: The dirt road to the park turns off the Cabot Trail in the village of North River Bridge, 16 km (10 mi) north of Exit 11 off Highway #105 and 35 km (22 mi) from Baddeck. There are signs on both sides of the road. Drive 5 km (3 mi) up the dirt road, which ends at the trailhead. A large sign with a map is located at the entrance to the woods.

Introduction: In the mid-1880s, this valley was home to several families of Highland Scots, who attempted to farm and raise livestock on the unrewarding soil. McLean, McKenzie, McLeod, and McAskill are still familiar names in Cape Breton, but the homesteads of the North River Valley have long been abandoned. Remnants may still be found along the trail, and the park is located on the former site of a school house and tannery.

This is an extremely demanding hike, long and with numerous scrambles up narrow paths clinging to steep slopes. Your reward, should you persevere, is an unparalleled view of the highest waterfall in Nova Scotia, 32 m (105 ft).

Trail Description: From the parking lot, the trail starts

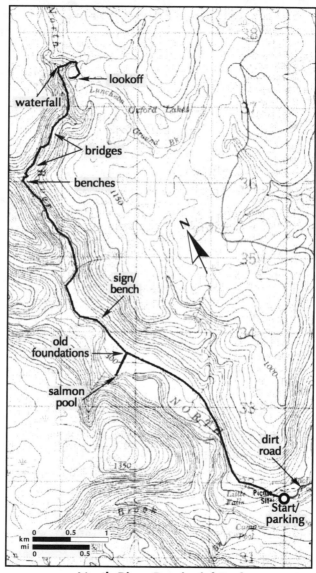

North River Provincial Park

just past the large sign containing a map of the path system. For the first 100 m/yd you hike uphill to connect to the former road. Beware of numerous side-trails cut by fishermen to access nearby salmon pools; rectangular red metal strips affixed to trees mark the proper route. For casual hikers, the first 5 km (3 mi) will make an enjoyable excursion. The trail follows the old road along the steep slopes of the gorge, ascending and descending between intervales that sheltered the early settlers. Except when crossing a few wet patches, it is comfortable walking for two side by side, with numerous sturdy bridges crossing the roughest ravines. North River can be heard rather than seen, and the hills towering overhead are particularly spectacular in October when the leaves change colour.

After crossing a large bridge, the trail gradually descends toward river level. A junction at a small clearing provides the opportunity for a diversion. Turn left and walk for perhaps 200 m/yd to arrive at a salmon pool underneath one of the highest hills in the area. A wonderful spot to rest and enjoy the surroundings, it is a good turn-around point for casual walkers.

Turn right, however, to continue along the main trail. Notice house foundations and stone walls underneath their white spruce covering. The path narrows beyond the remains of the homesteads, as it heads into more rugged terrain. After a few hundred metres a bench provides a resting spot beside the river, and a map signpost shows that the remaining few kilometres will be far more challenging. After this bench, roots and rocks frequently invade the trail, which zigzags along the hill as the stream crowds to the edge of the steep slopes on either side. Handrails become more common, as both safety features and helpers in climbing, and bridges over the little feeder streams take on a decidedly homemade appearance. Expect to find some parts of the trail washed away, requiring short, agile detours.

North River shrinks as various tributaries branch off into their own canyons. The path follows the East Branch the final 3 km (1.75 mi) to the waterfall. Opposite the confluence with John MacLeods Brook, about 1.5 km (1 mi) from the end of the hike, two benches occupy a small clearing, and just past here is the first of two major bridges. Well-constructed structures lie at both remaining crossings, but between them, part of the trail follows the rocks of the river bank. In summer that is adequate, but during spring runoff it is a very dangerous spot. Guard rails become fewer and slopes steeper, and you may be forgiven if you think the route was designed by a mountain goat.

The last kilometre seems to be continuous steep climbs and drops, but any fatigue you feel should disappear when you sight the magnificent waterfall. The main trail leads to a small pool nearly underneath the cascade, and a 1-km (.5-mi) extremely challenging side trip climbs to a dramatic lookoff above the falls. Near the summit you encounter an unsigned junction with a connecting trail cut by snowmobilers. Turn right; the lookoff is perhaps 75 m/yd away. You must return along the same route you hiked in. This trail should be planned as a full day's activity to be really appreciated.

Cautionary Notes: Rugged and rocky, this trail will require adequate hiking boots. There is no water supply after the start, and you should not attempt this walk without some food.

Weather is highly variable, and showers can occur anytime; flurries in May or October are not uncommon. Runoff from the late-melting snow of the Highlands makes this walk potentially dangerous in March and April. In the summer, expect high humidity in the ravine.

Because of the heavy runoff, the bridges frequently suffer damage from overflowing streams. Check ahead of time to make sure the trail is open.

Cell Phone Coverage: For most of the trail no signal can be obtained. Some signal is received near the trailhead and on the top of the lookoff above the falls, but weaker phones will not be able to complete a call.

Future Plans: The Nova Scotia Department of Natural Resources hopes to eventually construct a loop trail system including several no-service wilderness camping sites within the confines of North River Park. A 4334-ha (10,709-a) tract of land surrounding and including the park has been restricted from future development under the Wilderness Area Protection Act, 1998. The DNR plans to develop a management policy that will probably include increased recreational usage, depending upon environmental and community concerns.

Further Information: A brochure, *Provincial Hiking Trails of Victoria County*, can be obtained by contacting the Department of Natural Resources.

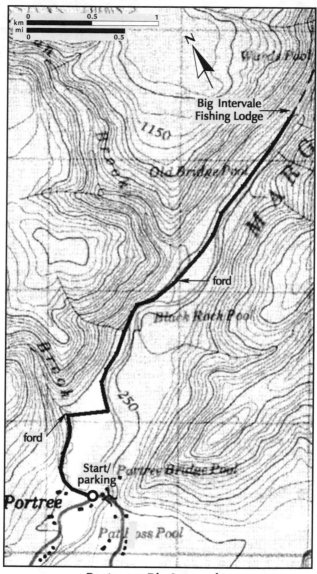

Portree – Big Intervale

Portree – Big Intervale

Length: 8 km (5 mi) return
Time: 2-3 hr
Type: dirt road, footpath, riverbank
Rating (1-5): 3

Uses: hiking
Facilities: none

Gov't Topo Map: St. Anns Harbour 11 K/7
Trailhead GPS Reference: N 46° 24" 03.7' W 60° 57" 57.0'

Access Information: At Margaree Valley, 4.5 km (2.5 mi) off Cabot Trail and 45 km (28 mi) northwest of Baddeck, turn right onto the paved road to East Big Intervale and Portree. After 700 m/yd, continue to follow the paved road, turning left. Avoid the dirt road straight ahead. Continue for 4 km (2.5 mi), crossing a one-lane bridge over the Northeast Margaree River. The trailhead is about 50 m/yd beyond the bridge on the right; park opposite the mailbox for M. Ross.

Introduction: The Margaree Valley, one of the most beautiful in Nova Scotia, is extremely interesting from a physiographic point of view. Numerous fault lines, wide varieties of geological strata, and the deep valley closely bounded by steep hillsides provide both scenery and study opportunities. One of the more impressive views is Sugarloaf Mountain, a large granitic intrusion rising more than 460 m (1500 ft). Recently sheltered under the Wilderness Area Protection Act, Sugarloaf separates the Margaree Valley into two narrow passageways, one of which provides our hike.

Originally profiled in the 1975 book *Walk Cape Breton*, the Portree – Big Intervale trail follows a former cart track through a narrow river gorge. Despite the poor

The Big Intervale Fishing Lodge at the end of the Portree–Big Intervale Trail.

condition of the treadway, this is definitely a worthwhile hike for the more experienced. Novices may be disconcerted by the thick young trees growing up in the former roadbed and uncomfortable fording the two large brooks that cross the route.

A pleasant recent addition is the Big Intervale Fishing Lodge, operated by a young Swiss couple. Located at the far end of the hike and open year round, the restaurant at the lodge makes an agreeable destination and a suitable stop for a brief rest and refreshment.

Trail Description: The former cart track begins over a low rise just past the driveway to house #12 and is partially obscured by vegetation. Do not follow the distinct dirt road uphill to the left. The path heads gently downwards, a low ridge developing on the left and broad open fields, pasture for both horses and cattle, on the right. Once past the fence, the old road, now used only by animals, becomes extremely wet and muddy. However, the track remains distinct, despite deadfall, alders, and erosion from drainage from the steep slope, and it traces the bottom of the hillside as it curves around the field. Lavis Brook flows on your right, slightly below you, and separates you from the animals in the field.

At nearly 800 m/yd, the brook turns sharply left into the hills, cutting directly across your route; it must be forded. Either continue straight and follow the former path — you'll have to walk in neighbouring fields because the original route is completely overgrown — or turn right and follow a row of fence posts until it reaches the bank of the river. I recommend this latter route. At the river, you obtain an incredible view of Sugarloaf, directly opposite, and of the narrow valley upstream, which is your route. Take a moment to chat with any anglers you meet. Some travel from distant parts of the world to fish for salmon in the Margaree Valley.

Turn left and follow the field to its northern end, where the old road re-enters the forest. The trail is raised about 3 m/yd above water level and separated from the land closest to the river by a false brook. Mostly hardwood trees surround you, but a fringe of softwood lines the Margaree. At 2 km (1.25 mi), you emerge from the woods on the riverbank near Black Rock Pool, where the road is completely eroded away. Scrabble over the rocks for the next 200 m/yd until you notice a small opening in the trees where the road starts again, the river curving right toward the hills opposite.

Only 200 m/yd further into the woods, you encounter a junction. You might continue straight along the former road, but it becomes extremely difficult to follow. Young trees cover the treadway thickly, limiting vision and slowing the pace to a crawl. On this path you reach MacLean Brook after 400 m/yd, but the bridge is gone, so it must be forded. After another 400 m/yd of bushwhacking, the trail reconnects with the other path at a junction beside the river.

Instead of following the cart track, you might turn right and explore the other route. This narrows into a footpath winding through softwoods fairly close to the Northeast Margaree. It shows evidence of being a watercourse during runoff, but it is fairly distinct. At MacLean Brook you must ford, and on the far bank the path becomes less easy to distinguish, skirting the western edge of a small semi-clear meadow. If you lose the path, turn right (east), and head toward the river. At the far end of the meadow you should find a distinct trail. Turn left, and follow the footpath past the remains of an old homestead and about 500 m/yd further to a junction with the old road, which will be on your left.

From the junction, follow the path as it gradually widens into a dirt track and, after 700 m/yd, a gravelled road. On your left are several cabins, and directly ahead is the Big Intervale Fishing Lodge. I recommend you stop and have a coffee or meal, then retrace your route back to your car.

Cautionary Notes: Hunting is permitted on these lands. Most of the land in the valley is private property. The right-of-way is restricted to very little space on either side of the former road. Please respect the right of access.

The trail is often overgrown and difficult to follow. If you lose contact with the path, walk southeast until you reach the river, and follow it southwest to return to the Portree Bridge.

Cell Phone Coverage: No signal can be obtained any-where on this hike.

Future Plans: A local community group is considering resurrecting the former trail, but no work had been started by 1998.

Tenerife Mountain

Length: 4 km (2.5 mi) return
Time: 2-3 hr.
Type: footpath, rocky slope
Rating (1-5): 4 (rugged terrain, steepness)

Uses: hiking
Facilities: none

Gov't Topo Map: Dingwall 11 K/16
Trailhead GPS Reference: N 46° 54" 27.0', W 60° 30" 56.2'

Access Information: From the village of Cape North, drive 4.5 km (2.75 mi) toward Bay St. Lawrence and Meat Cove. Look on your left for house #785, which is set back about 50 m/yd from the road. The footpath to the mountain begins between it and the unnumbered house on its right. Park on the highway opposite the houses.

Introduction: Tenerife Mountain may provide the most impressive view in Nova Scotia, and it would make any list of top ten favourite hikes. Of course, this is also one of the more difficult climbs available in the province. However, I think you will agree that the rewards are worth it.

No one in the area seems to know how Tenerife Mountain was named. The best explanation I have heard was that a local merchant captain, returning from a visit to the Canary Islands, decided that the high, steep hills of the Aspy Fault reminded him of that distant port.

The path actually begins between two houses, one belonging in 1998 to Hugh Buchanan and the other to Terry Campbell. They have no problem with anyone

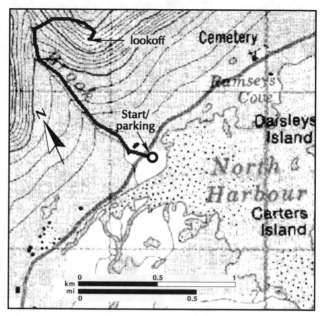

Tenerife Mountain

crossing their property and climbing the mountain, as long as you respect their property and carry out your garbage. Your destination is unmistakable, a bald hill rising nearly vertically behind their houses.

Ask Terry Campbell if you can buy some delicious "fresh-picked" crab when you are there. This tasty treat is almost sufficient reason to visit Cape North, whether you hike or not.

Trail Description: The footpath is distinct but unsigned. It immediately starts to climb, gently at first, through fairly young mixed forest. You soon hear Johns Brook on your left, although it remains unseen for some time. About 100 m/yd into the trees, a small path branches left. Continue straight; the peak of Tenerife beckons you through the leaves.

For the next several hundred metres, the trail parallels Johns Brook as it ascends into a deep notch scoured into the wall of North Mountain. Visible at times through the vegetation, the peak of Tenerife actually passes behind you as you climb. Occasional scraps of flagging tape and orange flashes on trees provide some reassurance that you are on the right route.

After about 750 m/yd, the trail turns sharply right and begins the real climb. At first the undergrowth is a little thicker, and young spruce almost obscure the path. This obstruction soon clears as the ascent becomes much steeper. You move into an area of young birch and beech, the undergrowth disappears, and the trail becomes confusing because the ground is almost nothing but rocks.

Your calves should be burning by now as you slow to a breathless trudge, the slope becoming steeper with each step. At about 1.5 km (1 mi), the vegetation begins to thin, and you can see the Aspy Valley behind and beneath you and the notch carved by Johns Brook on the slope opposite. Looser rocks and talus strew the treadway, and a massive rock overhang looms directly above you over the trees.

The final push is the most challenging, a precarious scramble over the bare face of the slope, where only a few mountain ash struggle up through the litter of rocks, to a saddle connecting the exposed knoll to its parent ridge. Once there, the full glory of your surround-ings becomes apparent. The view below is of the entire Aspy River Valley. To the southeast is White Point and Dingwall, with its gypsum pits. Lost in the mists to the southwest is the head of the valley in the national park. You can see far out into the Cabot Strait, possibly even sighting the ferry to Newfoundland. The thin, gleaming strip of the beaches at the head of Aspy Bay, stretching more than 10 km (6 mi), can be seen from end to end.

Local residents have placed a Canadian flag at the summit of the knoll. It is easily visible from the road below and acted like a magnet to me to climb this particular mountain. There is also a jar at the base of the flag, and people are encouraged to write their impressions of the climb on the notepad inside. Australians, Germans, and local citizens have all made the arduous ascent. One gentleman, aged 45, said that he required two difficult hours to make it to the top, but that the view made it all worthwhile and that he plans to return, no matter how long it takes.

You actually do not reach the highest point of the North Mountain range; Tenerife is only an exposed spur that is completely bare of vegetation. The ridge extends upward onto the plateau for the adventurous, but you will find no better view than from the top of this knoll. For most, therefore, I recommend spending a few minutes recovering your strength, then returning by the route you climbed.

Cautionary Notes: The climb is extremely steep, and frequent stops for rests should be expected. Carry plenty of water, even on a cool day.

Near the top the trail requires scrabbling over loose rock on a steep slope. Proper footwear is essential, and beware of knocking rocks loose to fall onto people coming behind.

The winds at the top can be extremely strong, and the summit is a relatively small area at the top of a very long fall.

Hunting is permitted on these lands, and poaching occurs throughout the year.

Cell Phone Coverage: No signal is available at the trailhead or on the approach climb. At the summit, a weak signal can be received that may be sufficient for more powerful phones. Climbing higher up North Mountain, you can obtain a stronger signal.

Future Plans: The North of Smokey Development Association and the Nova Scotia Department of Environment hope eventually to construct a 100-km (62-mi) hiking trail around the entire Polletts Cove – Aspy Fault region north of Cape Breton Highlands National Park. Tenerife Mountain is included in this proposal, which will create one of the finest backpacking excursions in North America.

Usige Ban Falls Provincial Park

Length: 7 km. (4.25 miles) return
time: 2-3 hr
Type: walking paths
Rating (1-5): 1

Uses: hiking, cross-country skiing
Facilities: outhouses, tables, covered tables, garbage cans

Gov't Topo Map: Baddeck 11 K/2
Trailhead GPS Reference: N 46° 12" 13.1' W 60° 46" 40.6'

Access Information: From Highway 105 take Baddeck Exit 9. Signs indicating the park direct you north toward Forks Baddeck. The falls are 15 km (9.25 mi) from Baddeck. Turn right on a dirt road just after crossing the Baddeck River. Follow the dirt road 3 km (2 mi) to the park, which is on your left.

Introduction: At the end of the Mesozoic era, 65 million years ago, all the land in the Maritimes was near sea level. The area now called the Cape Breton Highlands was

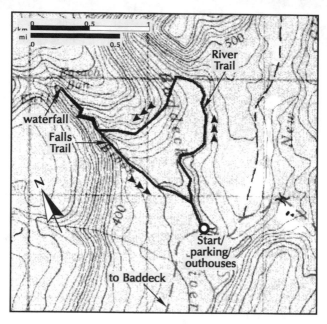

Usige Ban Falls

suddenly (in geological terms) uplifted 500 m (1600 ft), separated from neighbouring land forms by precipitous cliffs. Over the millennia, these cliffs have become deeply eroded, cut by narrow steep-sided ravines that provide drainage for the soil-poor heights. Waterfalls are common at the edge of the scarp slopes, and drainage valleys are often covered with talus (rocky debris) produced by freeze-thaw action. High rainfall, 1400-1600 mm (55-63 in) annually, and frequent low-level clouds or fog ensure relatively high humidity. Most of the Highlands area receives about 400 cm (13 ft) of snow each year, and spring thaw occurs later than in other parts of the province.

Usige (pronounced *ush-ka*) Ban, is Gaelic for "white

water," and if you walk to the base of this 15-m (50-ft) waterfall after a heavy rain, you will understand why it received that name. At the southern edge of the Cape Breton Highlands, Falls Brook is one of the many small streams permitting run-off from the plateau to escape. April and May are the months of heaviest flow, and the volume then would startle anyone who has only seen it in August.

The park also contains an area of climax hardwood, with many 200-year-old maple and birch. Considering that fewer than 1% of Nova Scotia's trees are older than 100 years, this is a rare treat.

This trail is similar to the longer and more challenging North River hike. However, although smaller than North River Falls, Usige Ban is no less beautiful and makes a worthwhile addition to any itinerary. Expect to find crowds of walkers on the trail on warm, sunny summer days; this is one of the busiest trails in Cape Breton outside the National Park.

Trail Description: A large map sign at the trailhead shows the lengths of each segment of the walk. Initially the path is well-gravelled and wide enough for two people to walk side-by-side. Roots and rocks have been covered by a thick treadway of crushed stone. For the first 250 m/yd there is only one path, high on the bluffs, with the North Branch Baddeck River on the right. At the first junction, turn right and follow the River Trail.

Descending a small hill, cross the bridge over Falls Brook and climb a small spur on the other side. The trail follows the North Branch Baddeck River for almost a kilometre, often descending to water level, at times climbing as much as 10 m (33 ft) above it. Generally, this is fairly easy walking, except for one steep switchback at the head of a bend in the river. A handrail provides assistance there.

The woods throughout this section are extraordinary. Mixed at first, but mostly hardwood once the trail turns inland, many maple and birch are over 100 years old. The canopy they spread ensures a sheltered walk, even on the hottest day. With the frequent cascades in the river and the numerous benches, this is an extremely pleasant walk, ideal for families. Turning almost 180 degrees as it moves inland, the trail follows the ridge line back toward Falls Brook. With good views in all directions thanks to a low understory, this 700 m/yd stretch is the hike's easiest walking. Once again, note the older trees, not all that common in Nova Scotia.

The River Trail connects to the Falls Trail perhaps 500 m/yd downstream from the cataract, crossing the creek over a sturdy bridge. This final distance demands a bit more effort, with more than 100 m (330 ft) of climbing required, most of that in the final 300 m/yd of the trail. As you approach the falls, its noise will drown out all other sounds. Crossing again to the north bank, round one more hill and you are suddenly at the base of the waterfall. A small bench is available should you need a rest or simply wish to enjoy the view, which is impressive. Resist any temptation to climb above the trail limits; there is no safe route beyond this point.

To return to the parking lot, retrace the route, but, at the junction, remain on the south side of Falls Brook on the Falls Trail. This path will follow the watercourse through lovely hardwoods until it reaches the North Branch Baddeck River, where both trails combine to climb the bluffs for the final 250 m/yd of the hike. Once again expect to find frequent benches along a level, easy walking path.

Cautionary Notes: After heavy rains, water flow in the brook can increase dramatically and suddenly. Be careful approaching the foot of the falls and do not scale the slippery surrounding rocks. It is for good reason that there is no path there.

Cell Phone Coverage: Coverage is good throughout, and calling is even possible at the base of the waterfall, although only if you turn and point the aerial downstream toward Baddeck. You are almost completely encircled by high cliffs at this spot and probably couldn't hear anything because of the noise of the water in any case.

Further Information: A brochure, *Provincial Hiking Trails of Victoria County*, can be obtained by contacting: Parks and Recreation Division, Department of Natural Resources, R.R. 1, Belmont NS B0M 1C0.

White Point

Length: 6 km (3.75 mi) return
Time: 2 hr
Type: dirt road, footpath
Rating (1-5): 2

Uses: hiking
Facilities: none

Gov't Topo Map: Dingwall 11 K/16
Trailhead GPS Reference: N 46⁰ 52 35.4' W 60° 21" 09.1'

Access Information: From Neils Harbour, drive 13 km (8 mi) along the Cabot Trail toward Cape North and Dingwall. Road signs indicate the turnoff on the right near the bottom of a long descent toward the ocean. Follow the unnumbered road for 14 km (8.75 mi), turning left and dropping sharply for 1.5 km (1 mi) to the village of White Point. At end of the paved road, by mail-

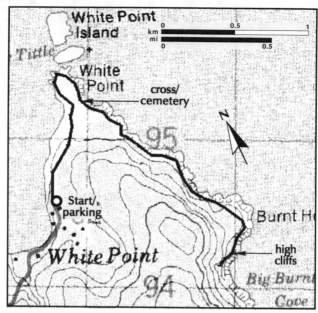

White Point

box #2119, continue straight up the dirt road for less than 100 m/yd, parking your car in the wider area. The trail is a continuation of the road.

Introduction: White Point may provide the most dramatic coastal scenery to be seen from any trail in Cape Breton. From its favoured position on the southern end of Aspy Bay, the grand sweep of both the beaches at the mouth of the Aspy River and the stark ridge of North Mountain across the far skyline are comfortably visible, as is St. Paul Island, the northern outpost of Nova Scotia.

The original English grantee was James Fitzgerald, in 1825, but White Point was the site of a French fishing village before that. The community's first church was established in 1872, a lobster factory by 1904, a school in 1920, and a sawmill in 1922.

Trail Description: For the first 500 m/yd the trail is a dirt road paralleling the slope of White Point Hill. As you move along the grassy hillside, thick white spruce crowd your right. The view to the left is magnificent: the rugged coastline from White Point to Black Head and the long, sandy South Harbour Beach to Dingwall Harbour. Cutting across the northern horizon is the natural wall created by the Aspy Fault, ending at Money Point. As you gently climb and round the hill, distinct paths branch in nearly every very possible direction over the grassy headland. Stay on what appears to be the main road as it climbs a small knoll, moving completely away from any vegetation except grasses and short, rugged shrubs such as juniper.

Continue straight down the gentle slope toward the thin point extending brazenly into Aspy Bay. A lone white cross beckons you forward; your path is a carpet of aromatic green liberally sprinkled with white granite rocks. When you approach the small knoll where the cross is located, you will see that the area in front of it is fenced off. This was the cemetery of the old French fishing village, the stone foundations of which can be found all over the end of White Point. A sign marks one of the grave sites: The Unknown Sailor.

Continue the few metres to the end of the point; White Point Island and its population of noisy gulls and terns is separated by a narrow passage called the Tittle. If you wish, you can scamper down the rocks to the narrow beach below, but the going can be difficult. Imagine, if you can, the fishers docking their small boats on a blustery day and climbing these slopes in driving rain.

Turn right and follow the Gulf of St. Lawrence coastline. The trail along the eastern shore is very stony, only becoming clearly defined near the water's edge at the base of the barren tip of White Point. You will begin to notice splashes of red paint on many of the rocks, especially as you near the trees. These mark your route for the remainder of the trip to Big Burnt Head Cove. The path moves down to follow the edge of the rocky coast, skirting the treeline as well. At the first marshy area, near a small indentation in the coast, driftwood and debris have been used to build a makeshift bridge.

Not long past this wet area the trail splits, with the painted rocks, which you should follow, heading left and closer to the ocean. Extremely rugged, this coastline is all harsh angles and large rocks, sometimes quite high above water level. Although the vegetation occasionally gets thick, especially at the head of tiny inlets which are sheltered from the wind, the path remains distinct, and splashes of paint will soon become apparent, although they are smaller and more weathered than previous markings.

The approach to Burnt Head is distinctive, the trail climbing through a notch between two barren knolls. Between those small rises, the wind whistles even more wildly in your face, and at the summit you see Big Burnt Head Cove in front and to your right. You are now more than 15 m (50 ft) above the water, and the entire coastline through this area is cliff. Often the path skirts within inches of the edge. Be extremely attentive of your footing because there are no guard rails. The trail continues only about 200 m/yd further, ending in thick vegetation before reaching the head of the cove. The painted flashes continue, but the brush is too thick to proceed beyond this point.

Turn around and retrace your route back to the base of the barren tip of White Point. Turn left, and climb the knoll in front of you. At the top, you will see the main trail, which you can follow to return to your car.

Cautionary Notes: The entire hike is on an exposed headland. During high winds and storms the temperature will be much lower than inland, and waves can break savagely on the rocks. Carry warm clothing except on the very warmest summer days.

Please restrict yourself to recognized footpaths. The vegetation on the point is quite fragile and can easily be disturbed by the many visitors.

Cell Phone Coverage: From the trailhead to the start of the barren headland you will not receive a signal. However, once you move past the higher hills and while following the coastline to Big Burnt Head Cove, all phones should be able to receive and transmit.

Future Plans: A local community group plans to improve signage and develop some interpretive panels.

Further Information: This hike is mentioned in David Lawley's book, *A Nature and Hiking Guide to Cape Breton's Cabot Trail*.

At Northern Head, Cape Percé, thick grass and moss often overhang the deeply eroded cliff edge.

NORTHEASTERN REGION

The Northeastern region, made up of the Cape Breton Regional Municipality along with Cape Dauphin and Boularderie Island, includes the most populous areas on Cape Breton Island. Few hiking opportunities can be found near the larger towns, partly because of the number of smaller communities clustered nearby but also due to the massive industrial activities associated with coal and steel.

A number of excellent trails are available in this area for novice hikers, young people, and those with limited mobility. Three small provincial parks near Sydney offer enjoyable marked walking paths; these are included in the Provincial Parks profile. Mira River Provinicial Park, with its many kilometres of riverbank, is a wonderful spot to walk during hunting season. Two Rivers Wildlife Park has not only an improved hiking track but much more available for the non-hiker as well. The path to the Fairy Hole is also a short walk but far more physically demanding; the Fairy Hole has been a destination for local residents for generations. The cave is an impressive sight, but the close views of the Bird Islands will interest almost as many hikers. True birders, however, will definitely want to visit Cape Percé. The number of species regularly sighted along this grassy headland is phenomenal, and the area has long attracted enthusiasts.

The Fortress of Louisbourg National Historic Site, the largest historical re-creation in North America, also includes within its boundaries many kilometres of unspoiled coastline, part of which the Kennington Cove and the Lighthouse Point trails follow. Both are quite challenging, but neither compares with the effort required to complete either the Cape Breton or the Gabarus – Belfrey Gut hike. The former includes the easternmost tip of Cape Breton Island, while the latter will take you along one of the most beautiful stretches of coastline you can find. Although many woods roads can be found throughout the area, the East Bay Hills trail is one of the better routes to follow for a longer hike through the interior and can be expanded easily for an extended trip. It is most suitable for experienced outdoors people.

Hunting is permitted in the areas of the Fairy Hole, Cape Breton, Gabarus – Belfrey Gut, and East Bay Hills trails. Hunting season usually starts around the first of October but varies from year to year and according to species. Contact the Nova Scotia Department of Natural Resources for detailed information before going into the woods. Although hunting is not permitted on Sundays, wear bright orange every day in season for safety's sake.

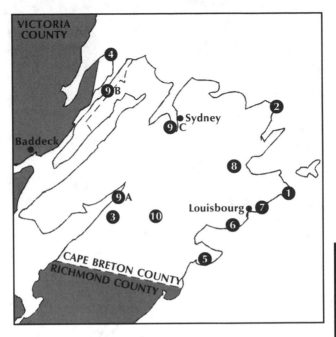

NORTHEASTERN REGION

Northeastern

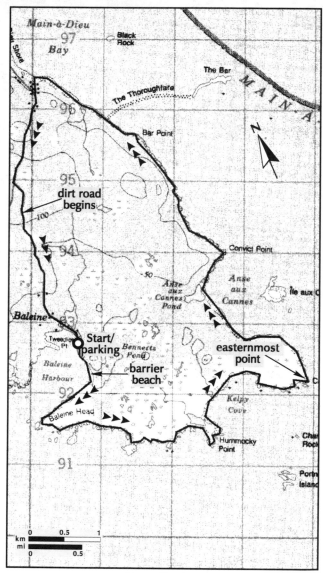

Cape Breton

Cape Breton

Length: 18 km
(11.25 mi) return
Time: 6 hr
Type: walking paths,
sand beaches, cobble
beaches, dirt road,
highway
Rating (1-5): 5 (distance,
rugged terrain, weather)

Uses: hiking
Facilities: none

Gov't Topo Map: Louisbourg 11 G/13
Trailhead GPS Reference: N 45° 57" 17.7' W 59° 49" 45.5'

Access Information: From Sydney, drive on Highway 22 toward Louisbourg for approximately 25 km (15.5 mi). At Catalone, turn left on the unnumbered road toward Main-à-Dieu. After 5 km (3 mi) you will reach the ocean at Bateston. Turn right. Reaching Main-à-Dieu, turn right at the intersection at water's edge and drive south toward Louisbourg for 4.5 km (2.75 mi). The dirt road to Baleine is on the left near the summit of a hill. Follow it until it ends, 3 km (1.75 mi) later, on a small hill overlooking a barrier beach.

Introduction: The easternmost tip of Cape Breton, this exposed headland gives its name to the entire island. The highly eroded bedrock surface is almost flat and is thickly covered in glacial till, sand, and gravel. Bogs and swamps dominate the poorly drained landscape, and balsam fir, larch, and spruce cling to the thin sustenance found in the poor soil. Around Baleine, rare arctic-alpine plants such as roseroot and fir clubmoss survive in the harsh, cool conditions.

Spanish fishermen were coming to Baleine as early as

the 16th century, but it was the English who first built a fort here, in 1629; it was destroyed that same year. No permanent settlement was erected until French settlers arrived in 1714. These in turn were supplanted by English colonists after the destruction of Louisbourg in 1758. Main-à-Dieu, French for "hand of god" and pronounced locally as "Manadoo," actually derived its name from the Mi'kmaq word *mendoo*, or "spirit of evil." This village, too, became English after French military power was destroyed in 1763.

Trail Description: The hike starts on a small rise above a rocky barrier beach separating Bennetts Pond from Baleine Harbour. The houses in the tiny village seem fragile protection when the surf is pounding and the wind blustering, which is often. Walking along the cobbled beach, watch for ducks sheltering in the fresh water on your left. In winter, lack of snow makes this area an excellent wintering spot for deer. At the other end of the beach, a distinct track continues along the shore. Actually, this entire hike requires few navigation skills; just follow the water's edge. Reaching Baleine Head, on a clear day you might be able to sight Fortress Louisbourg to the southwest. In 1725, the ship *Le Chameau*, arriving from France, went down on this rugged, rocky point with a loss of 310 lives and the pay for the garrison of New France. The wreck and most of the treasure were found in 1965.

Most people like to hike on sunny days, but I think that raw, blustery days are best for Atlantic coastline walks. Only then does the overwhelming and intoxicating power of the sea become apparent, the grey waves pounding the rocks with a deafening roar. On a sunny, calm day, the ocean is deceptive, beautiful and seemingly benign. For more than 7 km (4.25 mi) your hike continues along this bleak headland. Every twist and turn may hide tiny inlets, cobble beaches, and cliff walls, each spectacular and exciting. At Hummocky Point, a large brackish pond is protected behind the rocky projection. Stay close to the ocean's edge; trying to bypass the pond inland leads you into muddy, thick underbrush. From Hummocky Point you can see Cape Breton, the barren headland across Kelpy Cove. Crossing the cobble and sand covering Kelpy Beach, you reach (apart from a few islands) the easternmost tip of Nova Scotia.

Turning west into Anse aux Cannes, low hills give protection from the prevailing wind and trees start growing taller. Instead of barrens and brush, the woods come right to the beach's edge. Only Ile aux Cannes sits bereft of trees, the guano from seabirds having killed them. Waves are far less ferocious along this stretch, and it is warmer. Reaching Convict Point, about 3 km (1.75 mi) from Cape Breton, you gain a better view of Scatarie Island. Home to twelve fishing families as late as 1942, today it is a provincial wildlife sanctuary. Arctic hare and rock ptarmigan have been introduced, the only habitat of these species in the Maritimes, and they do quite well. Seabirds such as northern gannet are commonly sighted.

From Convict Point, perhaps 4 km (2.5 mi) of wooded walking remain. Main-à-Dieu Passage, often busy with little boats, separates you and Scatarie. A distinct path runs along the forest's edge, and the coastline is now high, jagged cliff until near Bar Point, where you will also find some old foundation sites and abandoned fields. The houses of Main-à-Dieu are quite clear now, and the trail actually ends by an old shed on a dirt road at the water's edge. Follow the road uphill to the pavement, and then left on the Baleine Road and your car, 4.5 km (2.75 mi) away.

Cautionary Notes: Expect variable weather conditions,

usually wind, fog, or rain, particularly on the Baleine side. This is an entirely unsupervised area with no signs or services, and the trails are not maintained. Before beginning your hike inform someone where you will be and when you can be expected back. Be prepared for emergencies.

Hunting is permitted on these lands.

Cell Phone Coverage: No call is possible at the start, nor until you reach Cape Breton itself. The signal becomes stronger as you approach Main-à-Dieu, although it disappears in some coves and near rock faces. There is good coverage at Main-à-Dieu and all along the paved road.

Further Information: Large boardwalks have been built around Main-à-Dieu Bay, and the Moque Head trail north of that village has been developed. The Cape Breton trail is listed in a booklet produced by the County of Cape Breton, *Trackdown: Trails in Cape Breton County*.

Cape Percé

Length: 8.5 km (5.25 mi) return
Time: 2-3 hr
Type: gravel road, dirt road, footpath, pavement
Rating (1-5): 2

Uses: hiking, biking, horseback riding, ATVs
Facilities: none

Gov't Topo Map: Glace Bay 11 J/4
Trailhead GPS Reference: N 46° 10" 40.9' W 59° 50" 31.1'

Access Information: From Sydney, follow Highway 4

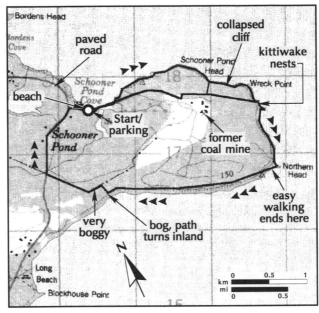

Cape Percé

toward Glace Bay. At 12 km (7.5 mi), take the Donkin – Port Morien turnoff (Dominion Street) and drive 4 km (2.5 mi) to the junction with Highway 255 (Brookside Street). Turn right, and drive 6 km (3.75 mi) on Highway 255 to the junction with an unnumbered road. Highway 255 turns right; continue straight on the unnumbered road and drive 6 km (3.75 mi) through the village of Donkin. The road to Cape Percé is the first gravel road on the left by Schooner Pond Cove.

Introduction: Cape Percé may be one of the best places on Cape Breton to watch birds. The marshes of Schooner Pond hide so many different species that I have heard of one birder who keeps a separate list just for this area. When I walked there in July 1998, I saw four kestrels and five goshawks in the air at one time circling over the broad, grassy fields. Black-legged kittiwakes, small gulls that usually nest on offshore islands, maintain a small colony on the cliffs near Wreck Point.

In the centre of Cape Percé you will find the remains of a coal mine that was active until the 1980s. Huge seams of coal run far out under the ocean throughout this part of Cape Breton, and the first coal mining operation in North America was located on the outskirts of nearby Port Morien in 1720.

Trail Description: Cross over the small brook draining Schooner Pond and follow the road until you reach the end of the beach. A distinct ATV trail leads up the grassy hill on your left; follow it as it traces the outline of Schooner Pond Head more than 15 m (50 ft) above the ocean. A wide, level grass fringe extends between the stunted trees on your right and the cliff edge. Very easy walking, with a tremendous view out into the Atlantic, the trail gently leads right around the headland.

As you round Schooner Point, the next headland, Wreck Point, will be at the limit of your view, with tiny Flint Island and its forlorn lighthouse visible about 4 km (2.5 mi) out to sea. Watch the water below you closely; seals are common, chasing fish quite close to shore, and they will often take a moment to look you over before submerging again. About 300 m/yd beyond Schooner Pond Head the ATV trail turns into the forest to detour around an area where the cliff has collapsed. Walking across this 500 m/yd section, however, is very easy, and it provides one of the few points where you might actually be able to descend to the water. The hillside is terraced like a giant's staircase, with long horizontal ridges, each several metres lower than the next, all the way to the ocean. At the bottom, there are piles of flat, square slate stones looking like nothing else than massive cookies.

On the far side of the collapsed section the cliff resumes as your route follows the coastline around Wreck Point. Looking at the base of the hillside, you should be able to find jet black deposits of coal peeking through the brown sandstone and siltstone. For a short distance the path is for walking only, but once around Wreck Point, near two narrow fingers of rock extending toward Flint Island, the ATV trail rejoins it. Now much broader and obviously very heavily used, the path heads southward toward Northern Head. Watch carefully for black-legged kittiwakes, small gull-like birds that nest on the cliff wall around here. This is one of the few mainland locations where you will be able to find their nests. The grassy fringe on which you have walked from near the start of the trail begins to narrow, and the thick white spruce crowds outward almost to the edge of the cliff. Fortunately, the ATV track provides easy passage through the dense vegetation, although it sometimes comes very close to the eroding edge.

Northern Head is the final headland before the trail turns 90° right and heads toward Morien Bay. Be extremely cautious: the large grass and moss carpet overhangs the deeply eroded cliff edge, providing no warning of the precipitous drop-off. The soft soils of the edge may not be able to bear your weight. You will also notice massive fissure lines in the field where the soft rocks are splitting away from the hillside due to the pounding of the waves. South Head is the long peninsula in view across Morien Bay, and the community of Port Morien can be seen about 6 km (3.75 mi) up the bay. Scatarie Island is visible beyond South Head.

Most walkers should turn back at this point, returning to the first ATV trail near Wreck Point and following it inland. After a short walk through lovely softwood forest, keeping left at all junctions, you emerge near the abandoned mine buildings. Follow the gravel road about 1 km

(.5 mi) back to your car at Schooner Pond Cove, taking a moment to inspect the old reservoir and dam on your left just above the pond.

Those more hardy may wish to follow the path beyond Northern Head. It becomes much rougher, with vegetation intrusions and frequent deadfalls obstructing the treadway. Substantial wet areas must be negotiated as well, as the narrow trail works through the spruce forests lining the hillside. However, the trail should be relatively simple to identify until shortly after you return to grassy open spaces. The path becomes progressively more difficult to distinguish, so stay close to the waterline if you become confused. Before you reach the farm silo, you encounter a marshy clearing. Turn right on a narrow path heading inland. Once beyond the marsh, the trail widens and conducts you to a power line. Turn left, and follow the ATV track through substantial boggy areas back to the paved road. Turn right; your car is about 1.5 km (1 mi) along the road.

Cautionary Notes: The entire coastline is high, almost vertical cliff. Be very careful near the edges.

There is no signage. Beyond Northern Head the trail should be attempted only by experienced hikers. When the path turns from the coast toward the power line, you are almost bushwhacking.

Cell Phone Coverage: A strong signal was received throughout the hike. No dead areas were detected.

Further Information: Profiled for several pages in Pat O'Neil's book, *Explore Cape Breton*.

East Bay Hills

Length: 26 km
  (16.25 mi) return
Time: 7-10 hr
Type: dirt road
Rating (1-5): 5 (distance;
  navigation skills required)

Uses: hiking, biking,
  horseback riding, ATVs,
  snowmobiling
Facilities: none

Gov't Topo Map: Mira River 11 F/16, Grand Narrows
  11 F/15
Trailhead GPS Reference: N 45° 58" 44.8' W 60° 25" 50.0'

Access Information: From Sydney, drive 22 km (13.75 mi) on Highway 4 toward St. Peter's. The trailhead is left across road from houses #4978 and #4980. Park your car on the grassy verge just off the highway, not blocking the road up the hill. Ben Eoin ski hill is 600 m/ yd past the trailhead on Highway 4.

Introduction: Long distance hikes in the interior of Cape Breton County are difficult to find, and many of them are extremely wet. Because of the flat or rolling topography throughout much of this part of Cape Breton Island and the sandy or stony glacial till thinly overlying the bedrock, low ridges separated by poorly drained depressions are common, and the scenic quality tends to be low. The old road across the top of the East Bay Hills is an exception, although there are still many wet areas, particularly on the plateau.

This is a good route for anyone who wants a full day hike or an overnight tramp close to Sydney. I have recommended turning around at the Breac Brook Bridge and returning to Ben Eoin, but if you have two cars you can leave one by the Big Pond District 14 Volunteer Fire Department, only 1 km (.5 mi) further along Highway 4.

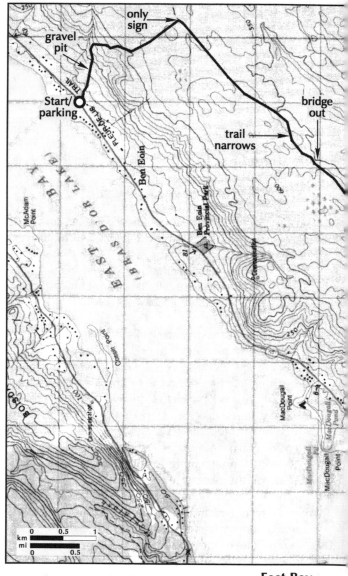

only sign

gravel pit

Start/ parking

TRAIL

FLEUR-DE-LIS

Bon Eoin

bridge out

trail narrows

EAST BAY (BRAS D'OR LAKE)

McAdam Point

Ocean Point

Ben Eoin Provincial Park

Communication

Communication

MacDougall Point

MacDougall Rd

MacDougall Pond

MacDougall Point

km
0   0.5   1
mi
0   0.5

East Bay

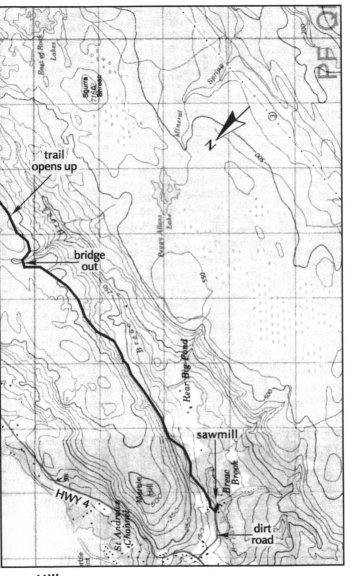

Hills

The trail would become a 14 km (8.75 mi) hike, re-quiring perhaps 4-6 hours.

Trail Description: A wide gravel road climbs uphill from the start. Follow it, ignoring the frequent ATV side paths in these first few hundred metres. Crossing a little brook, the track gets rougher, and it reaches an abandoned gravel pit after 600 m/yd. This is the best view of the entire hike, the Boisdale Hills across East Bay of Bras d'Or Lake.

Past the gravel pit the treadway becomes much rockier and the trees older and thicker. Climbing steeply, the road switches back and forth, mostly through hard-woods, for 1.5 km (1 mi), passing a distinct side trail 1 km (.5 mi) from the start. Near the crest, in level areas, there will almost always be ponds in the middle of the old road which demand short detours through the brush. Barely 100 m/yd past the highest point of your climb, you reach the T-junction with the old road crossing the top of the East Bay Hills. A small sign on one of the trees points to Ben Eoin, back the way you came, and Big Pond, to your right. This is the only sign on the entire route, but it is an extremely important one.

Because of the heavy ATV traffic, the old road is wide, easy to follow, and muddy. Paralleling the broad plateau on the top of the East Bay Hills, your route will be nearly level for the next 4 km (2.5 mi), climbing and falling within a 15-m (50-ft) range. About 500 m/yd from the Ben Eoin turnoff, you reach another prominent junction, this one unsigned; turn right. Once past that, the treadway becomes grassier. After a further 300 m/yd a swamp, on your right, drains over the track, requiring an ankle-deep ford.

One of the nicest sections of the walk begins just past the swamp as the trail gently climbs through a thick stand of young spruce. Another junction, 600 m/yd further, requires taking the right fork, the much more distinct path. Now descending, you proceed through lovely spruce and on dry treadway until you reach what appears to be a vehicle turn-around. After that, the woods close in, the brush not having been cut back as it was in earlier sections. Rapidly becoming much wetter, the trail nevertheless remains clear until you reach an un-bridged brook about 5 km (3 mi) into the hike. For the next 1.5 km (1 mi), after crossing the brook, vegetation almost blocks the path, although it does remain easy to follow.

Suddenly you emerge into the open. Once again the trees have been cleared back from the edge of the route, much further back than at any point thus far. For the re-mainder of the hike you will have no shade, and the track will gradually transform into a vehicle route. At 7 km (4.25 mi) you cross another stream, the road veering right to conform to the ravine it has cut. Again, there is no bridge, but it will be easy to cross at any time other than after heavy rainfall. Within 500 m/yd, the treadway becomes gravel, and you consistently lose elevation. Breac Brook Valley is quite conspicuous on your left, and ahead you should be able to see the hills sur-rounding Big Pond.

Fields appear on the left slope, and you should sight the first buildings. You have excellent views of the wide, almost deserted valley as the path stays nearly 60 m (200 ft) above the creekbed. At 10 km (6.25 mi) an old road heads left to hunting cabins on Breac Brook, and at 11.5 km (7.25 mi) the first residence, #280, with a Cape Breton Post delivery box, is also on your left. De-scending steadily now on the wide gravelled track, you reach the bridge over Breac Brook 1.5 km (1 mi) later, on the left, having passed the junction with the road to Big Pond.

Have lunch beside the creek, then retrace your route

back to Ben Eoin or continue along the road to Big Pond and the car you left there.

Cautionary Notes: Hunting is permitted on these lands. There is very little signage, and you are travelling through a fairly isolated area. Be certain to inform someone where you have gone and when you expect to return.

Cell Phone Coverage: Coverage is very strong at Ben Eoin. The signal weakens the closer you get to Big Pond, although stronger phones can probably always complete a call. By the time you emerge from the thickest vegetated area onto clearer roadway, about 9 km (5.5 mi) into the hike, weaker phones probably will not be able to make a connection.

Future Plans: This old road may become part of a long-distance ATV trail running from the Canso Causeway to Sydney.

Further Information: Contact the Recreation Department of the Cape Breton Regional Municipality for details about their route from the East Bay Community Centre.

Fairy Hole

Length: 4 km (2.75 mi) return
time: 1-2 hr
Type: footpath, steep slopes, rocky cobble
Rating (1-5): 3 (rugged terrain)

Uses: hiking
Facilities: none

Gov't Topo Map: Bras d'Or 11 K/8
Trailhead GPS Reference: N 46° 20" 32.2', W 60° 25" 15.2'

Access Information: From Sydney, drive 40 km (25 mi) east along Highway 125 and Highway 105 to Seal Island Bridge. About 1 km (.5 mi) after the bridge, turn right onto New Harris Forks Road. Follow the dirt road for 5 km (3 mi), turning right at the stop sign. Continue until the road ends 12 km (7.5 mi) later by a shed numbered #2576 and #2578. Park here; do not block the driveway or the entrance to the shed.

Introduction: Long a popular walk for local residents, the path to the Fairy Hole is known as "the trail of the Little People" by the Mi'kmaq. The cave itself is reputed to be *Kukmijnawe'nuk*, or "the place of my grandmother," where Glooscap, the man-god, retired from the outside world. The native peoples always travelled this trail in single file to protect the delicate land from too much human intrusion.

Situated on the northern tip of Kellys Mountain, a separate elongated block of the Cape Breton Highlands running between St. Anns Bay and the Great Bras d'Or Channel, this is a surprisingly difficult walk. It is not maintained; deadfall, steep hillsides, eroding cliffs, and slippery rocks make this a challenge for children and

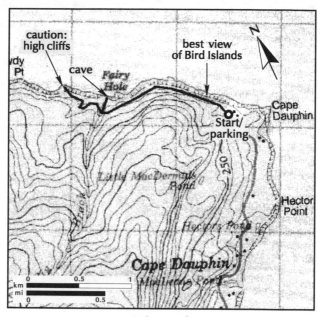

Fairy Hole

less mobile individuals. It is definitely a worthwhile destination, but be prepared to spend longer than you expect to approach it safely.

Trail Description: The trail is a narrow footpath starting to the left of the shed. A tiny brook runs beside the track, which crosses a small field before entering the predominantly softwood forest. Hills rise immediately on both sides, and your course becomes very rough as it scrabbles over rocky intrusions and gains elevation. Very early you also encounter the first of many trees that have fallen across the path. In the thin soil of Kellys Mountain, roots cannot run deep, and the hurricane-force winds of large storms knock over new victims frequently. Unlike in a park, no one clears this path, so dozens of these natural barricades must be negotiated before you reach your destination.

By 500 m/yd, you have passed between the knolls and the ocean becomes visible through the trees on your right. The Bird Islands, Hertford and Ciboux, lie just off Cape Dauphin, and from the path you get an excellent view. The treadway improves for a short time, clear and distinct as it heads gently downhill, and it appears as if many of the stones have been moved to the sides. However, in a few moments you face more thick deadfall, requiring either a detour or some agility.

Because of the frequent obstacles, several well-worn paths sometimes work their way through the forest. Watch for occasional scraps of orange flagging tape in the trees to mark the main trail. Little more than 1 km (.5 mi) from the trailhead you come upon an indistinct junction. The right fork takes you down a narrow path that descends the steep side of the ravine bordering Big Brook. The left fork continues high on the ridge for another 100 m/yd before more easily moving downward to the creek. Whichever path you choose, turn right at the bottom of the deep gorge, and follow the water over slippery stones to the tiny cobble beach at the mouth of Big Brook.

On your right, ropes affixed to the dark rock wall lead a further 20 m/yd to the Fairy Hole, a cavern burrowed by waves into the face of the cliff. Large enough for anyone to enter, the cave widens inside and is said to extend for a considerable distance into the hillside. I did not explore it, nor do I recommend that the average hiker do so. You might have to get your feet wet to reach the cave, and you should be cautious about entering the Fairy Hole if the tide is coming in. The entrance lies below the high tide mark, and you might be trapped and drown.

Returning to the trailhead from here results in a walk

of less than 3 km (1.75 mi). If, instead, you follow Big Brook back to the trail junction, you will notice that the path continues up the hill on the far slope. Following the ridge line initially, it passes through hardwood trees, reaching another ravine about 300 m/yd further on. Crossing over the dry creek bed and climbing the hill on the opposite bank, the footpath is well marked by flagging tape. At first heading toward the ocean, the trail suddenly turns 90° left to end in a stand of spruce trees on the top of a 15 m (50 ft) cliff, with a magnificent view of the Highlands coastline toward Cape Smokey. The Bird Islands are also well silhouetted, and the rugged coastal cliffs of Cape Dauphin make a lovely photograph.

Retrace your path to the junction, turn right, and make your way back to the car.

Cautionary Notes: At high tide, the water level rises to cover the approach to the Fairy Hole. During storms, waves break powerfully over the beach. Before you go there, find out which way the tide will be running.

Do not attempt to explore the far reaches of the Fairy Hole. Caving requires specialized skills and equipment.

Footing in Big Brook is rocky and slippery, and the hillside approach is vertical and extremely uneven. This trail is not recommended for young children or anyone with limited mobility.

The trail ends on a 15-m (50-ft) cliff with a crumbling edge obscured by vegetation.

Cell Phone Coverage: Coverage is complex and variable. At trailhead there is a strong signal, but within 500 m/yd, as soon as you pass behind the first small knoll, it fades to nearly nothing. At the bottom of Big Brook, no signal can be obtained, but a weak signal is found on the beach, and calls may be possible from

The rugged shoreline at Cape Dauphin. The Fairy Hole is at the bottom of these cliffs.

just outside the Fairy Hole. At the trail end on the high cliff, a weak signal could be acquired.

Further Information: This trail is outlined in *Explore Cape Breton*, by Pat O'Neil.

Gabarus – Belfry Gut

Length: 40 km (25 mi)
return
Time: 10-12 hr
Type: former road,
walking paths, rock
beaches, sand beaches,
ATV tracks
Rating(1-5): 5 (distance)

Uses: hiking, mountain
biking, cross-country
skiing, ATVs, snow-
mobiling, horseback
riding
Facilities: none

Gov't Topo Map: Mira River 11 F/16
Trailhead GPS Reference: N 45° 49" 38.7' W 60° 08" 15.0'

Access Information: From Sydney, follow Highway 327
to Gabarus, about 35 km (22 mi). Drive through the
village until the pavement the ends by the breakwater,
and turn right onto the dirt road until it ends in a parking
lot beside a cemetery. The trail starts on the far side of
the parking lot and is a former road, no longer maintained.

Introduction: This unbelievable coastal walk is the longest hike in this book. There are numerous spectacular
camping opportunities along the route, and the chance
of seeing wildlife is good. The barrier beach system
around Winging Point is one of the most extensive in the
province, permitting the experienced hiker to extend
this into a several-day excursion.

The last person moved out of Gull Cove in the early
part of this century, leaving behind several foundations,
stone walls, old fields, and the former road connecting it
to Gabarus. You can find the names of the families who
lived there in the graveyard by the church at the start of
the hike.

Trail Description: Your route, starting on the far side of the parking lot, is the former cart track connecting Gabarus and Gull Cove. Now used by ATVs, it offers quite easy walking despite many wet areas. Comprised entirely of granite chewed to till by glacier action, this region is relatively flat, has practically no soil cover, and is poorly drained.

The first 2.5 km (1.5 mi) is very wet throughout the year as it skirts Harris Lake through an extensive bog. Fortunately, the ATV people have built a bridge over the brook from Rush Lake, although you may wish they had also ditched the road. Early problems will be forgotten when you reach the coast. You emerge at the far end of Harris Beach, a typical barrier beach of rock and till separating ocean and freshwater. The lake, though small, is deep enough for swimming and can be quite warm. Loons nest there. It is a gorgeous spot, and I have camped on the grassy headland near where the trail comes out of the woods.

The route now follows the coastline closely. Between Harris Beach and Lowell Point you find a stone fence on your right near an old field, and there is another just past Lowell Point as well. With the harsh weather conditions of the area, it takes longer for the forest to reclaim these fields and clearings. After 4 km (2.5 mi), you arrive at Hardys Point and Gull Cove. The woods give way to a substantial expanse of cleared land on the slope of Bull Hill, and on the far side of the cove are a chain of sea cliffs, the only ones along this part of the coast.

A number of stone walls and house foundations may be found in the tall grasses. The area is also fairly sheltered from the wind and a good spot for a picnic. Because of the low snowfall, this is valuable winter habitat for deer. Expect to see at least one somewhere in the area. During migratory season, numerous birds

ford

sand
beach

possible ford/
alternate parking

Gabarus –

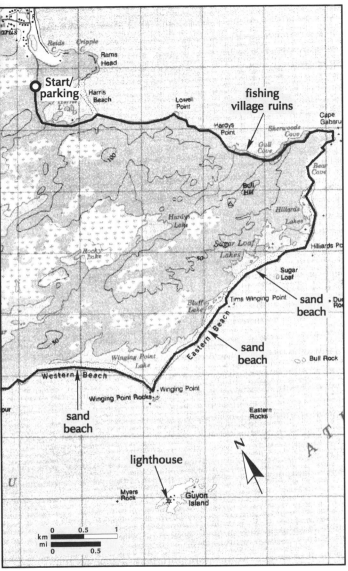

Belfrey Gut

use Fourchu Bay as a staging area, and this coastline is an important breeding territory for seabirds. On Green Island, visible from Cape Gabarus, exists the only large nesting colony of black-legged kittiwake known in the Maritimes. For many people, this is a good place to complete the outbound hike and turn back.

However, you can extend the hike along the shore for another 15 km (9.25 mi). ATV trails cut across Cape Gabarus and emerge at Bear Cove. From there, continuous cobble and till beach systems stretch all the way to Belfry Gut on Fourchu Bay. Until Hilliards Point you are walking mostly on rock; afterward, for more than 10 km (6.25 mi), virtually all your hike is on sandy beach. This is a spectacular area of barachois ponds enclosed by barrier beaches, and Winging Point, less than 10 km (6.25 mi) beyond Gull Cove, is worth making the trip for by itself.

Past Gull Cove conditions become harsher and more variable. In stormy weather, some of the barrier beaches, especially the eastern beach of Winging Point, are swept by waves and provide no protection. The stream draining Little Harbour Lake, waist deep in the spring, must be forded. The further you travel along this route, the more isolated from assistance you become. With the exception of the lighthouse on Guyon Island, you will see no human structures until you reach Belfry Beach. Only very experienced backpackers should attempt this trip, and only after notifying authorities of their intentions. If you do hike the entire distance, however, you will love it.

Cautionary Notes: There is no signage on this hike, nor are any services, such as water, available. Remember that exposed coastline is cooler and windier than the interior.

Belfry Gut, the only exit for the waters from Belfry

Lake and Gabarus Lake, is forever changing. When I visited in the summer, it was a slow-moving channel perhaps five metres wide and one metre deep, that I easily waded. In the fall, it had completely silted over and at low tide could be walked without getting wet feet. If you intend to end your hike here, check conditions first.

Hunting is permitted on these lands.

Cell Phone Coverage: No signal is available in Gabarus, but as you head toward Cape Gabarus it gains in strength with calls possible on the high ground around Gull Cove. A weak signal persists to the end of Western Beach, Winging Point, but then fades away as you approach Belfry Beach.

Future Plans: 4413 ha (10,900 a) in the Gabarus area were sheltered under the recently passed Wilderness Areas Protection Act. Over the next several years a management policy for these lands will be developed.

Further Information: Free copies of the system plan for parks and protected areas can be obtained from the Nova Scotia Department of Natural Resources.

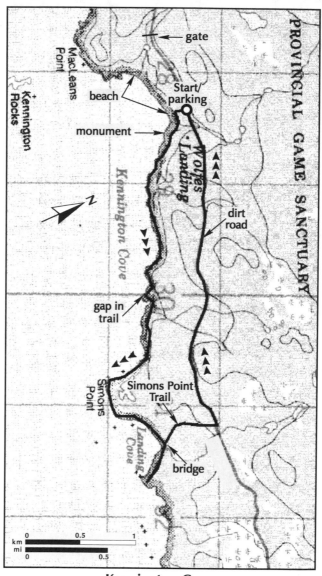

Kennington Cove

Kennington Cove

Length: 8 km (5 mi)
  return
Time: 2-3 hr
Type: footpath, rocky
  beach, gravel road
Rating (1-5): 3

Uses: hiking
Facilities: garbage cans,
  tables, washrooms,
  supervised beach, water

Gov't Topo Map: Mira River 11 F/16
Trailhead GPS Reference: N 45° 52" 47.9' W 60° 03" 20.5'

Access Information: Entering Louisbourg on Highway 22 from Sydney, drive along its main street until you reach a fountain, where you turn right. Watch for the sign indicating Kennington Cove. Drive 5.5 km (3.5 mi), mostly on dirt road, to a stop sign next to a parking lot in clear view of the fortress. Turn right here, and turn right onto a gravel road 500 m/yd later at the next road junction. Continue straight at the next intersection, 900 m/yd further. Follow the road for another 5 km (3 mi) to the parking area at Kennington Beach. Park on the left; the trail starts to the left of the beach.

Introduction: This lovely cove received its latest name from the warship HMS *Kennington*, which took part in the final English capture of Fortress Louisbourg. Earlier names include Freshwater Cove and Anse de la Cormorandière (Cormorant Cove). In both sieges the initial landing of the attacking forces was made on these beaches. In 1745, the French defended this area with only a small detachment; in 1757 they built and garrisoned extensive field works here.

Scottish immigrants settled here in the early 19th century to farm and fish. A lobster cannery opened in 1896 and operated until the 1930s; Gaelic church services

Northeastern

were conducted at the Presbyterian Church until 1948. The final 16 residents moved when their land was expropriated in the 1960s.

This area is both a national historic site and a provincial game sanctuary. Hunting is not permitted, nor is camping without prior approval. The sand of the beach is exceptionally light coloured because of quartz derived from the nearby rocks.

Trail Description: From the parking area, walk across the field and down the hill to the left of the beach to the series of small bridges and boardwalks crossing Kennington Cove Brook. A well-defined footpath climbs the grassy headland on the other side of the brook, passing old stone walls on your left. Just beyond the crest, you will find a substantial stone monument with a bronze plaque commemorating General James Wolfe's landing on June 8, 1758. It was erected in 1930, long before the national historic site was established.

Past the monument, the walkway is initially along the grassy fringe between the white spruce and the eroding edge of the coastline. For most of the walk there will be a 3-5 m (10-16 ft) coastal cliff, the thick layer of reddish-brown glacial till covering the land east of Kennington Cove being constantly washed away by the restless Atlantic waves. Soon, however, the path moves into areas of krummholz, coastal white spruce thickets shaped by wind and salt spray. You will notice branches growing into the route, making passage increasingly difficult. The first wet area, just after the monument, is crossed by the rotting remains of an old boardwalk, showing that this trail was abandoned some time ago.

Soon large deadfall obstructs your progress, and thick vegetation makes it difficult to distinguish the correct path. Novices should turn back, but the more nimble can drop down to beach level and follow the coastline.

The bridge at the mouth of Soapstone Brook.

The rocks on the shore are fairly large and irregularly shaped, but the beach is broad enough to permit a choice of footing for the first few hundred metres. As you approach the base of Simons Point, however, the coastal fringe narrows, the cliffs become higher, and deep indentations cut into bands of slate all the way to the foot of the hillside. Finally, you must make your way back up to the top of the hill, carefully scrambling up the loose soil. Once there, you will find reminders of the old trail, usually broken corduroy boardwalks.

For the next 500 m/yd you must slowly pick your way through the thick white spruce and deadfall on the hilltop, not at all a pleasant task. Your reward is in sight, however, as the open cobble of Simons Point, heavily populated with gulls and cormorants, beckons. Even before you reach the beach, a grassier fringe opens up between the tree boundary and the cliff edge, the slope lowers almost to sea level, and your route leads around a small barachois pond.

Rounding Simons Point, the trail curves into Landing Cove. You can probably see a bridge near the mouth of the brook at the head of the inlet, about 500 m/yd away. Before you reach Soapstone Brook and rejoin a well-maintained footpath, one or two difficult spots remain that require you to work through thicker vegetation, but most of the distance is on cobble or grass.

Crossing the bridge, you are able to continue about 400 m/yd to the eastern headland of Lowland Cove, the farthest point of your hike. The exposed headland in front of you, about 2 km (1.25 mi) away, is White Point. Although you could easily continue following the coastline, I recommend you turn back here, recross the bridge, and follow the distinct footpath as it heads inland through the spruce forest. There is no signage, but the track widens enough for two to walk side-by-side, and several new boardwalks conduct you across some of the worst wet areas.

The trail emerges onto the dirt road connecting the town of Louisbourg with Kennington Cove beside a shelter and the road bridge over Soapstone Brook, which a park sign calls Freshwater Brook. The path is signed as the Simons Point Trail. Turn left and follow the road 3 km (1.75 km) back to the Kennington Cove parking area.

Cautionary Notes: Weather conditions can be quite extreme, especially on exposed headlands. Anyone planning to make this hike should be dressed properly, with warm, waterproof clothing. At high tide and during storms, the beach portion of the walk between Wolfes Landing and Simons Point is not recommended.

The coastal cliffs are actively eroding and are composed of loose soils. Be careful when climbing on this uncertain footing.

Cell Phone Coverage: Coverage is quite weak. At the trailhead, I was unable to obtain any signal, nor can any signal be received until you reach Simons Point. Even there, weaker phones will not be able to make a connection. The signal disappears at Landing Cove and under vegetation; a weak signal was reacquired at some points along the road between Soapstone Brook and Kennington Cove.

Further Information: A number of books are available about Fortress Louisbourg, and the interpretive centre at the site contains fascinating displays.

Lighthouse Point

Length: 14.5 km (9 mi) return
Time: 5 hr
Type: footpath, rocks
Rating (1-5): 4 (rugged terrain)

Uses: hiking
Facilities: none

Gov't Topo Map: Louisbourg 11 G/13
Trailhead GPS Reference: N 45° 54" 24.8', W 59° 57" 26.0'

Access Information: Upon reaching Louisbourg on Highway 22, turn left on Havenside Road. There is a large Parks Canada sign visible only after you make the turn. Follow the narrow, winding paved road for 2 km (1.25 mi) past numerous residences. A large sign indicates that you have reached the Louisbourg Game Sanctuary; the road becomes dirt. Follow it for another 1.5 km (1 mi) to its end in a parking area near the lighthouse.

Introduction: Few trails offer such a combination of historical record and scenic magnificence. From the trailhead, the site of the first lighthouse in Canada (1734),

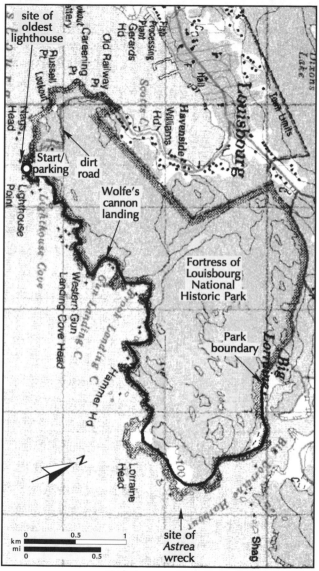

site of oldest lighthouse

Start/parking

dirt road

Wolfe's cannon landing

Fortress of Louisbourg National Historic Park

Park boundary

site of *Astrea* wreck

Lighthouse Point

through Gun Landing Cove, where British besiegers of Fortress Louisbourg landed artillery, to Lorraine Head, where the *Astrea* ran aground in the early 1800s with a loss of more than 500 lives, there is scarcely a square centimetre of ground that does not have some story. And the setting is phenomenal: restless, angry seas, jagged, rocky shoreline, and desolate, savage coastal barrens, set opposite the largest historical reconstruction in North America, Fortress Louisbourg.

People have been hiking this coastline for decades, and there is a well-worn footpath from Lighthouse Point to Big Lorraine. However, there have been no improvements to the natural track, nor will you find bridges, benches, or any of the other facilities you might expect on a trail in a national park. This is not a trail for everyone.

This area is both a national historic site and a provincial game sanctuary. Hunting is not permitted, nor is camping without prior approval.

Trail Description: The path begins at the parking lot by the lighthouse and follows the coastline eastwards. One of Parks Canada's familiar hiker signs indicates the way. I should mention that it also has the word DANGER posted underneath. This trail is a narrow footpath for much of its route, running close to a high cliff wall overlooking the ocean. For most of the remainder, it crosses exposed and slippery rock.

At the treeline, the path divides. The most heavily used direction is *not* the way you wish to go. That route drops down onto the rocks near the water level and forces you to scramble most of the next 500 metres over very slippery footing. It is where most people explore who only want to walk a few minutes away from their cars. The true hiking trail enters the thick white spruce, staying up above the shore and within the vegetation.

At about 750 m/yd, the narrow, rocky beach gives way to open coastal barren. The trail divides again, and one route hugs the vegetation boundary and cuts off the headland. The other, more interesting, follows the coastline. From it, you will see two Inukshuk on the top of small hills, put there by previous hikers.

Walking becomes much easier now, with softer earth making up the treadway. The sea wall is quite high and nearly vertical in this area; during rough weather the waves smash high over the rocks, drenching those who venture carelessly close. The coastline turns inward to Gun Landing Cove, where you cross a short cobble beach. At the far end, the path re-enters the forest and cuts behind the next headland, picking through dense white spruce and over uneven, rugged hills. Returning to the ocean at the head of Brook Landing Cove, you carefully pick your way over another cobble beach, past the outflow of tiny brooks.

From here, your route is almost completely in the open for the next 3 km (1.75 mi), following the edge of the coastline. Large knolls of granite thrust out of the green, mossy land, and the trail moves around them. Ghost-like dead trees, eerie guardians in the fog, cover some of the ocean-facing slopes as you approach Hammer Head. As you near Lorraine Head, the hills become higher and more intrusive, forcing the path to wind its way around their base. On the top of the point, some hiker nearly always sets up a marker of some kind to note his or her visit.

The final two kilometres are more difficult. Once Lorraine Head is rounded, the coast starts curving into Big Lorraine Harbour, the trees crowd in closer, and the space you have to walk in almost disappears. At one point, the trail actually vanishes, washed out by the relentless tidal action. Although it is possible to work around the washout by walking inside the tree line, the footing is difficult and the vegetation very thick, so for many this may be the end of the hike. However, if you are able to get past that tough 25 m/yd, the path becomes distinct again, and it follows the coast all the way around the edge of the harbour until you reach a brown house with yellow storm shutters. There you will find the end (or the beginning) of a dirt road and signs marking the park boundary.

You may retrace your route to get back to your car or follow the road inland back to Louisbourg.

Cautionary Notes: Weather conditions can be quite extreme, especially on exposed headlands. Anyone planning to make this hike should be properly dressed, with warm, waterproof clothing.

Some endurance is necessary to complete the rugged 14.5 km (9 mi) distance, and a certain amount of agility will be required to negotiate the rougher sections.

Cell Phone Coverage: Coverage is quite weak. At the trailhead, I was unable to obtain any signal until I climbed to the Lighthouse. On the trail I was unable to get a sufficient signal to transmit at water level, but I was able to transmit on the higher knolls.

Future Plans: In 1977, a two-volume proposal for a high-quality hiking trail was prepared for Parks Canada, but funds were never available to undertake its construction. Instead, the narrow path continues to be used by many enthusiasts every year.

Further Information: A number of books are available about Fortress Louisbourg, and the interpretive centre at the site contains fascinating displays.

Northeastern

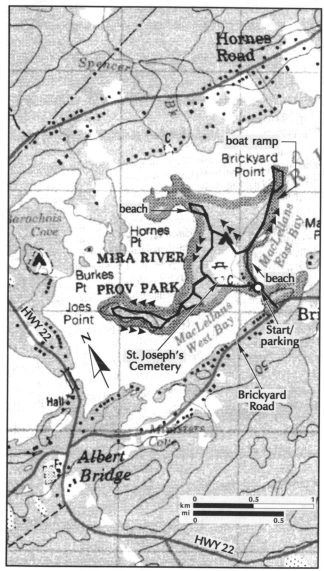

Mira River Provincial Park

Mira River Provincial Park

Length: 6.5 km (4 mi) return

Time: 1-1.5 hr

Type: paved road, gravel road, walking paths

Rating (1-5): 1

Uses: hiking, cross-country skiing

Facilities: outhouses, picnic tables, garbage cans, water, camping, playground, beach, boat launch

Gov't Topo Map: Sydney 11 K/1

Trailhead GPS Reference: N 46° 01" 37.3' W 60° 02" 16.9'

Access Information: From Exit 8 on Highway 125, drive 15 km (9.25 mi) on Highway 22 towards Louisbourg. Just after crossing the Mira River, turn left on Brickyard Road, indicated by a sign. Continue slightly more than 2 km (1.25 mi); the park entrance is on your left. Park your car at the gate.

Introduction: The Mira River has a special place in the folklore of Cape Breton. Situated in a long, narrow valley created along a fault line, the Mira River extends in a broad arc from Framboise Cove to Mira Gut. A thick layer of glacial till deposited in the last ice age covers the land on both sides of the river, and the sands and gravels form many small islands and peninsulas.

Mi'kmaq used the long waterway extensively and camped all along its length. In the early 1700s, French settlers established farms, and the remains of their efforts, abandoned fields and old apple trees, can still be found in the park. Brickyard Point, the site of the boat launch, received its name from the brick works that the French established there in 1727 to supply material for local settlers and the nearby Fortress of Louisbourg. After 1763, when the English gained control of Cape Breton,

Northeastern

large numbers of Irish and Scottish settlers moved into the area to farm the comparatively rich soil.

In recent times, the Mira River has become one of the favourite summer vacation areas for Cape Breton residents. Cottages line both banks, and boaters cruise up and down the river continuously. In addition to the provincial park camping area, scouts, guides, church groups, and private individuals maintain campgrounds on its popular shores. Walking in the park is quite easy; the trails have a wide treadway and virtually no change in elevation. I recommend hiking here after the park closes in October, when hunting season makes many other locations less comfortable. Suitable for all fitness levels, Mira River Provincial Park makes a very pleasant location for a late fall stroll.

Trail Description: Start your walk at the gate near the park entrance and follow the paved road over the narrow isthmus separating MacLellans West Bay from MacLellans East Bay. Turn right at the first junction and follow the road as it changes to gravel and passes by the large beach area. This is a very busy spot in the summer, but by fall the bay will contain only a few migratory birds. The camping area of the park is visible on your left on the other side of a fence. Continue on your present course, with occasional detours into picnic areas to the right, until you reach the boat launch at Brickyard Point.

The former road continues straight, but is now gated to prevent vehicles from proceeding. A footpath circles the narrow point, permitting shore access close to the small island just off the eastern tip. Tables are available for picnickers in the summer, and blueberries grow thick. The footpath reconnects to the gravel road at the boat ramp, and you must retrace your walk back toward the start for about 500 m/yd until you reach a gated maintenance road on your right. The service area for the campground is to the right of this. Follow that road past another gate, and turn right again. You are now in the camping area.

A dirt road leads past several campsites. Watch the numbers carefully, because when you reach site #79, on your right at the first sharp bend, a narrow footpath at the back connects you to site #144 through the woods. Turn right again, and the road ends less than 200 m/yd later at a small, unsupervised beach facing west at Hornes Point.

From here, return along the road through the campground. Continue following the right-hand track through the confusing maze of short loops. This will lead you to the longest dedicated walking path in the park, near site #107, the 1.4 km (.75 mi) loop around Joes Point, the western tip of this leaf-shaped peninsula. Unlike the gravelled park roads, grasses cover this treadway. The woods through here are quite attractive, many tall hardwoods providing a high protective canopy over a new generation of spruce and pine. The path actually does not lead you to the end of Joes Point, although you can see the river through the trees. Shortly before you rejoin the campground, look carefully to your right. A narrow footpath leads down to MacLellans West Bay and a small, isolated gravel beach.

Once back on the road, continue to take every right-hand turn until you reach the pavement. The campsites seem older here, and older spruce and larch dominate. Just after you pass the last campsite, on your left, you will find St. Joseph's Parish Cemetery, a fair-sized field surrounded by a brown picket fence. The earliest gravestone I could find was dated 1880, but the crosses pre-date that. A Roman Catholic burial site, it is still being used for new interments.

The final few hundred metres take you to the camp-

Northeastern

ground administration building, where you can find washrooms and a pay phone. From there, continue over a small hill to return to the gate at the park entrance and the end of your walk.

Cautionary Notes: none.

Cell Phone Coverage: There is marginal coverage, especially under thick forest cover and near the park entrance. Weaker phones may not be able to make a connection in some places.

Further Information: A brochure about Mira River Provincial Park can be obtained by contacting the Nova Scotia Department of Natural Resources.

Provincial Parks:
Ben Eoin, Dalem Lake, Petersfield

Length: 1.5 km (1 mi) return (Ben Eoin)
  2.5 km (1.5 mi) return (Dalem Lake)
  2 km (1.25 mi) return (Petersfield)

Time: 1 hr   **Uses:** hiking

Type: walking paths,   **Facilities:** washrooms,
  former dirt roads   tables, garbage cans,

Rating (1-5): 1   water

Gov't Topo Map: Mira River 11 F/16 (Ben Eoin)
  Sydney 11 K/1, Bras d'Or 11 K/8 (Dalem Lake)
  Sydney 11 K/1 (Petersfield)

Trailhead GPS Reference:
  N 45° 57" 43.8' W 60° 27" 34.6' (Ben Eoin)
  N 46° 15" 12.6' W 60° 25" 37.5' (Dalem Lake)
  N 46° 08" 41.8' W 60° 13" 16.0' (Petersfield)

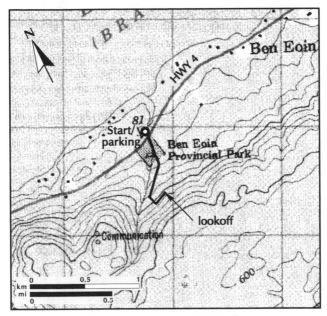

Ben Eoin Provincial Park

Access Information:

Ben Eoin: From Exit 6 on Highway 125, drive 25 km (15.5 mi) on Highway 4 towards St. Peter's. The park is on the left, and a road sign indicates the entrance. Continue past the gate to the grassy picnic area. The trailhead is near the washrooms.

Dalem Lake: From the junction of Highway 125 and Highway 105, drive 14 km (8.75 mi) towards Baddeck. At Exit 15, turn right onto St. James Road. Continue 800 m/yd to New Dominion Road. Turn left onto a dirt road, and continue for 1.3 km (.75 mi). Watch for the park entrance on the right, enter, and drive for a further

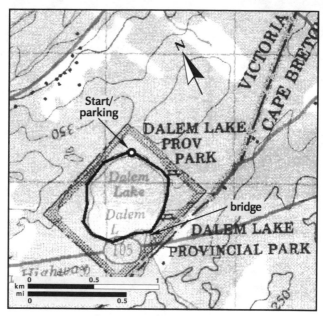

Dalem Lake Provincial Park

700 m/yd to the final parking area. Walk toward the lake; the trail runs between the parking lot and the beach.

Petersfield: Take Exit 5 off Highway 125. Head northeast for 4 km (2.5 mi) to Westmount Road (Highway 239). Turn right; drive for approximately 1 km (.6 mi). The park entrance is on the left.

Introduction: Near Sydney, there are a number of small provincial parks that offer short but worthwhile walks, especially for seniors, young families, and novices. Each of the three described here offers something different: Ben Eoin is a short climb to a lookoff over East Bay, Dalem Lake Trail is a loop encircling a small lake, and

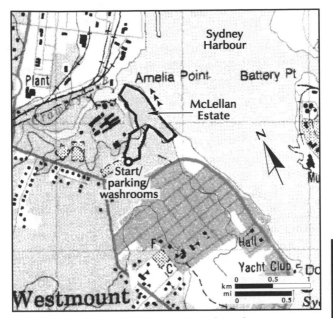

Petersfield Provincial Park

Petersfield is a maze of walking trails surrounded by urban development.

Trail Descriptions:

Ben Eoin, a 91 h (225 a) picnic ground located near the popular ski slope on the East Bay Hills, offers a quiet place to have lunch and a good opportunity for almost anybody to enjoy a short climb out of the park to a viewing site overlooking the Boisdale Hills across East Bay.

The trail is well marked by a metal sign on a post at the far end of the road which loops through the picnic grounds. You begin to ascend immediately, heading through mixed spruce and hardwoods. Wide and with good footing, the trail even has some old corduroy over wet spots. Initially climbing southeast, the trail switches back in the other direction when it reaches a bench and a park boundary sign and follows a ridge. The trees become mostly hardwood, and you can see the water of East Bay through the leaves. The slope also becomes steeper. Switching back and forth, the footpath continues over some small bridges crossing run-off channels. When the trail begins to level out, you know you have almost reached the end, a large rocky outcropping overlooking East Bay and the Boisdale Hills. Return the same way you climbed.

When the park is closed, you must begin your walk at the gate on the Highway 4. This adds about 400 m/yd to the walk.

Dalem Lake, a 74 h (183 a) property just inside Victoria County, presents a large beach and swimming area in addition to its picnic grounds. The trail runs around the lake just inside the trees, allowing easy observation of the water. As duck and loon are frequent visitors, this is a good walk for birders. Many species of warbler nest in the thick, young trees inside the park. Follow the path counterclockwise. While it is fairly level throughout, little mounds of earth make the treadway slightly uneven. Small corduroy bridges span the worst wet spots, and at the far end of the lake, in the middle of thick, young softwood, wood chips cushion stretches of the route.

You are very close to Highway 105 and can hear traffic. Once you have rounded the lake and are on your return, you will find a bench beside a small beach area connected to Highway 105 by a dirt track.

Shortly after you cross a fairly large bridge over Aconi (Fifes) Brook, you reconnect with the picnic grounds and beach area. The path continues parallel to the beach, inside the fringe of trees between the parking areas and the water.

Petersfield, only 23 h (57 a) in size, contains remnants of four cultural periods dating from the 18th to 20th centuries. The park is named after Colonel Samuel Peters, who was granted land near Point Amelia in 1787 after the War of American Independence. His property became known as "Peter's Field," and the name has remained to this day.

Any number of short paths can be combined at Petersfield. For the longest route, follow the boardwalk surrounding the parking lot to the grassy area at its far right end. Take the gravelled track heading across the field into the trees. Keep straight at the first junction, heading toward the McLennan Estate. Most junctions are well signed. Pass the caretaker's cottage on the former road and turn right at the next junction. You are in fields again, the remains of the estate grounds. Keep following the right hand path, and you will arrive at interpretive signs by the ruins of the estate's main buildings The signs outline the magnificent past of these beautiful fields. Head downhill to Sydney Harbour and follow the trail as it re-enters the trees. Walking around the tip of Point Amelia, your view changes from the busy industrial activities on the South Arm to the quiet waters of Crawleys Creek. Benches along here permit you to sit and watch whatever operations may be underway at the Coast Guard College.

Numerous alternative paths cut across the point and permit you to reconnect with almost any section of the park. Continuing right, your route leaves the harbour and heads gently uphill, entering an area of older hardwoods and crossing a seasonal creek over a small bridge with no railing. Turning through 90°, the path emerges at the upper left side of the parking area to complete the loop.

Cautionary Notes: Ben Eoin is a small park surrounded by private land. Hunting is permitted there between

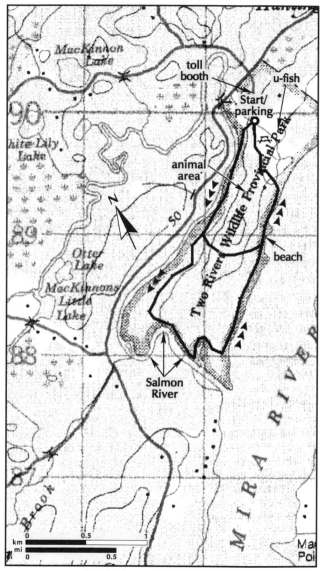

Two Rivers Wildlife Park

October and February. Wear orange when in the woods, even on Sundays when hunting is forbidden.

The beach at Dalem Lake is unsupervised.

Cell Phone Coverage: There is strong coverage through-out on all three trails.

Further Information: A brochure about Petersfield Park can be obtained by contacting the Nova Scotia Department of Natural Resources.

Two Rivers Wildlife Park

Length: 5 km (3 mi) return
Time: 1-2 hr
Type: walking paths
Rating (1-5): 1

Uses: hiking, cross-country skiing
Facilities: outhouses, water, garbage cans, picnic tables, benches, pop machines, playground

Gov't Topo Map: Mira River 11 F/16
Trailhead GPS Reference: N 45° 55" 47.9' W 60° 17" 55.9'

Access Information: On Highway 327 at Marion Bridge, watch for the sign indicating the park and turn right on an unnumbered paved road before you cross the Mira River. Drive 10 km (6.25 mi) on the paved road; the park entrance is on the left. There is a toll booth 200 m/yd in on the gravelled entrance road. The park fee in 1998 was $3.50 + HST. The parking lot is 500 m/yd past the toll booth. The trail entrance is at the top right corner of the parking lot.

Introduction: The grounds of Two Rivers Wildlife Park

have a recorded history nearly 300 years old, although Mi'kmaq are known to have used the area much earlier. Settled in the early 18th century, the ridge was occupied by a series of French farms and a sawmill, all of which were burned after the capture of Louisbourg in 1758. Resettled by Caleb Huntington almost 50 years later, the land was farmed by his family for nearly 200 years until the Province of Nova Scotia acquired it in 1971 and established Two Rivers Wildlife Park. A not-for-profit association began administering the facility in 1995 when it looked as if it would be closed because of government financial constraints; the group still operates Two Rivers.

Two hiking options are available: the Short Loop, about 2.5 km (1.5 mi), or the Long Loop, approximately 5 km (3 mi). Easy walking suitable for almost anyone, both trails are quite pleasant except for some very wet spots on the Long Loop. With the large picnic grounds, one of the few wildlife parks in the province, a swimming area, and the new U-fish, there are many activities to supplement the relatively short hike and more than enough to justify a visit.

Trail Description: Boardwalks surround the parking area, and, although no sign marks the trailhead, a large display board at the entrance to the wildlife area indicates the start location. Immediately the wide, gravelled path descends from the narrow ridge running through the centre of the park and joins up with the Salmon River, flowing on your right. You may notice directional arrows pointing the opposite way; the interpretive trail is designed to be walked clockwise. Large, round, numbered wooden signs mark the different interpretation stations.

Running parallel to the river through thick, young mixed woods, the trail is wide, level, and marked with flagging tape. Nylon ropes block frequent side paths entering on your left. A 25 m/yd corduroy boardwalk, ending at station #18, crosses a significant wet area, and on the far side the treadway becomes more natural, made up of soil and grasses. Moving inland and climbing slightly, you soon reach a junction. Turn left for the Short Loop; continue right for the Long Loop.

Through the forest on the Long Loop, the trail is wide and level with a good drainage ditch on the left. In the thick vegetation your view is limited. Do not get fooled at an unmarked junction a few hundred metres after the junction of the short and long loops; turn left on the better-defined path, and watch for scraps of yellow and orange flagging tape on the trees. Even in dry months much of this trail will be wet.

Working up a small hill, the path climbs a hardwood ridge before dropping down to reconnect with the Salmon River. Watch for a sign saying Use Caution Ahead. After this, the path descends rapidly, then turns sharply through several bends before heading left into a swampy area near the mouth of a small brook. Although some corduroy has been laid down and a small bridge constructed, washouts are common, so be prepared to squish through clinging black mud up to your ankles.

You should be able to sight some houses on the far bank of the Salmon River as the trail crosses the small undulations separating you from the Mira. When the trail curves left again, the broad river, almost 1 km (.5 mi) wide, comes into view on your right, the track approaching it quite closely. The path follows the river-bank, turning sharply inland once to climb a small hill. A rope barrier protects a lookoff over Huntington Bay, as this section of the river is called. At the top of the hill you encounter one more unpleasant wet area, and perhaps 20 m/yd beyond that the treadway becomes gravelled once again.

Much wider with no roots or rocks intruding, the trail

is comfortable walking for two side-by-side, and it parallels the Mira behind a narrow fringe of trees that protect you from the wind without blocking your view. Turning inland, the trail reconnects with the Short Loop in an area of white spruce. For most of the next kilometre you will enjoy very easy walking. Do not miss the short gravelled side trail about 25 m/yd past the junction on your right that leads downhill to a tiny barachois beach and a wonderful view of the Mira.

At station #3, the trail emerges from the forest into a large field. Follow the path as it climbs up the gentle ridge, intersecting with a road near the top. From here, you can turn left and head toward the park administration building and the wildlife area of the park, you can turn right and follow the road over the grassy field toward the picnic tables and U-fish, or you can continue straight back to the parking area and your car, about 400 m/yd further on.

Cautionary Notes: None.

Cell Phone Coverage: You are unlikely to receive any signal in the forested sections of the hike and only a very weak signal in the parking area or at higher elevations in the picnic grounds. Only the strongest phones are likely to work.

Future Plans: Continued improvements to the treadway are planned, including class-one gravel over the entire Long Loop. New, large historical interpretive panels will be installed.

Further Information: The park produces a brochure providing detail about the interpretive stations.

SOUTHEASTERN REGION

With the exception of the Port Hawkesbury trail, all the Southeastern Region trails are in Richmond County. Richmond County may be the least well known part of Cape Breton to outsiders. Inverness and Victoria counties have the Cabot Trail, Cape Breton Highlands National Park, and the Trans-Canada Highway. Cape Breton County has industrial and urban centres and Fortress Louisbourg. Visitors tend to hurry to these more famous locations, neglecting the southeast. I confess to this myself, never having hiked on any of the trails until 1994. Do not make the same mistake, because I found the scenery in Richmond just as exciting as anywhere else on Cape Breton, particularly along the coastline. And now that the road from Grand River to Fourchu and Sydney has been paved, access is much easier.

New hikers will appreciate the opportunities to test their legs on the short Cape George trail, which offers access to the Bras d'Or Lake shore, and on the well-defined footpaths in Lennox Passage Provincial Park. The pathways of Port Hawkesbury and St. Peter's Rail Trail – Battery Provincial Park, though longer in total, can be arranged to provide shorter distances if required and are both easy to follow. Delorier Island, while not an improved route, is an excellent site to walk along ocean coastline without encountering thick vegetation or difficult footing. Little River Reservoir can be suitable for families and those with limited mobility, especially if they remain on the road to the pumping station and on top of the earthen dam. Pringle Mountain is more suit-

Southeastern

able for experienced hikers only, requiring a strenuous climb and frequent wading through wet areas, but the view from the top of Sporting Mountain is quite pleasant.

The coastal perimeter of Richmond County is amazing, the glacial till of the south coast having been reworked by the Atlantic waves to create long barrier beaches over much of its length. Capelin Cove delighted me, perhaps the more for having been completely unexpected. Its wide coastal barrens and low relief provided long views in every direction. Point Michaud, with its long beaches and barachois ponds teeming with birdlife, is worth visiting with the entire family, although the hike might be a little long for younger children. Rugged Cape Auguet, on the southernmost tip of Isle Madame, is a challenging walk that will be most enjoyable to the experienced hiker.

Hunting is permitted in the areas of the Delorier Island, Capelin Cove, Cape Auguet, and Pringle Mountain trails. Hunting season usually starts around the first of October, but it varies from year to year and according to species. Contact the Nova Scotia Department of Natural Resources for detailed information before going into the woods. Although hunting is not permitted on Sundays, wear bright orange every day in season for safety's sake.

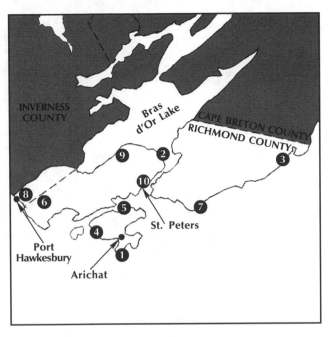

SOUTHEASTERN REGION

Southeastern

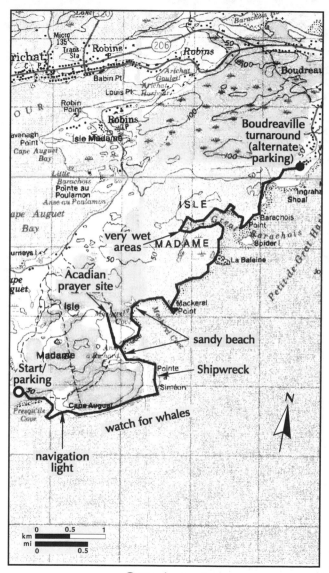

Cape Auguet

Cape Auguet

Length: 23 km (14.5 mi)
return
Time: 5-7 hr
Type: dirt road, footpath,
coastal barrens, beach
Rating (1-5): 5 (distance,
rugged terain)

Uses: hiking
Facilities: none

Gov't Topo Map: Chedabucto Bay 11 F/6, Cape
Canso 11 F/7
Trailhead GPS Reference: N 45° 28" 13.6' W 61° 01" 17.5'

Access Information: From Port Hawkesbury, leave Highway 104 at Exit 46, the junction with Highway 320. Turn right, and follow this road over the bridge onto Isle Madame. About 400 m/yd past the bridge, turn right and follow Highway 206 in the village of Arichat, turn right to Lower Road, then turn left and follow the paved road along the coast to the turnoff to Cape Auguet, posted also with a Clearwater sign. Turn right, and continue for 1.5 km (1 mi); watch for the Clearwater sign at the junction and turn left. Three kilometres (1.75 mi) further, you will reach a yield sign. Turn left onto the gravel road and follow this for 2 km (1.25 mi) to the Clearwater Lobster holding facility. The parking area is on the right before the gates.

Introduction: Like most of the coastline of Isle Madame, the small coves around Cape Auguet were settled predominantly by Acadian families who fished and farmed for subsistence. Ancestors of present day Boudreaus, Richards, Forests, LeBlancs, DeCostes, and Allens homesteaded in Anse à Bucket, Anse à Foret (Forest Cove), Anse aux Macquereaux (Mackerel Cove), and Anse à

The Cape Auguet Trail is a challenging walk along a beautiful, deserted stretch of coastline.

Richard. For 150 years these families scratched a meagre living from sea and soil, but their increasing isolation, a 16-km (10-mi) round trip walk to school, a 20-km (12.5-mi) walk to church, and daily rows to Petit-de-Grat or Arichat to sell the catch produced an accelerating out-migration. In 1913, the last two families left Anse aux Macquereaux for the larger communities, although the isolated coves were used extensively by rum-runners during prohibition in the 1920s, and sheep grazed the pastures in the 1930s and 1940s.

This is a challenging walk along a beautiful, deserted stretch of coastline. Until further development occurs, I recommend that only fit hikers undertake the full walk from the Clearwater plant to Boudreauville and return. At many points the trail is difficult to follow and there are frequent wet areas that must be crossed. Younger children and novices will not enjoy this hike, although once the treadway is enhanced it will be one walk that everyone will want to explore.

Trail Description: From the parking lot, walk left around the perimeter of the Clearwater plant until you reach the coastline. Just before the water's edge, you should notice a cut through thick white spruce. The narrow footpath leads to a large field covering the hillside above Presqu'ile Cove, with the remains of boundary fences and stone foundations of houses scattered about. Several tracks lead over Cape Hogan, the first headland, but I recommend staying close to the water and scrabbling over the rocky end of the point. Much more difficult than the grassy path over the top, this route is nevertheless one of my favourite places on this trail. The town of Canso is easily visible on a clear day, the ocean view is superb, and the wild wind at the point never fails to make my blood race.

As you round Cape Hogan, gradually climb toward the small navigational beacon at the top of the hill. You will reach it slightly more than 1 km (.5 mi) into the hike. Rejoin the footpath and follow it for the next kilometre as it manoeuvres in and out of the thick krummholz of densely packed white spruce close to the edge of the coastal cliff. You are quite high above the water and on the slope of an eroding hillside, so be cautious. Frequent wet areas must be endured, and intruding game trails sometimes appear to be the path. Watch for infrequent scraps of flagging tape and never go further than 10 m (30 ft) from the ocean.

At Guet Point, you walk onto a small area of grassy barren. On the far side of Petit-de-Grat Harbour are the lighthouse on Green Island and the community of Petit-de-Grat. The coast cuts left, and the footpath works through the brush another 700 m/yd to Anse à Richard, passing by the rusting remains of a wrecked schooner on a small beach. The beach at the head of the cove is wonderful, a small swath of sand sheltered by protective hills. Follow the remains of the cart track, now an ATV trail, up the next hill and about 700 m/yd inland. You will find, on your left, a cross enclosed by a white picket fence, a prayer area established by residents of the cove for occasions when they could not complete the long hike to church.

Return almost to Anse à Richard and follow the high ground left toward the headland separating it from Mackerel Cove. The hills gradually disappear, and by the time you reach Mackerel Cove you will be almost at ocean level. A barachois beach outlines the top of the cove, and rocky cobble makes up your footing as you round Mackerel Point and hike the next 1.5 km (1 mi) to the mouth of Great Barachois. Here the route cuts sharply left, detouring more than 1 km (.5 mi) through large wetland areas before reaching the top of this narrow inlet. This section will not be particularly enjoyable, but once on the other side you'll be on a distinct trail that leads up to Barachois Point, with its good view of nearby Spider Island. A dirt road leads the final kilometre into Boudreauville and emerges from the young, thick woods by house #258.

If you left a second car here, your walk is over. Otherwise, turn around and head back the way you came.

Cautionary Notes: Hunting is permitted on these lands.

There is no signage except occasional flagging tape, nor are there any services such as water. Exposed coastline is cooler and windier than the interior. Be prepared for extreme conditions and inform someone of the time you expect to return.

Cell Phone Coverage: A strong signal is received at the trailhead and until you reach Guet Point. From there on, weaker phones may not be able to complete a call near sea level, in thick vegetation, or in the shadow of hills. At higher elevations, such as the hills around Anse à Richard, all phones should work.

Future Plans: Development Isle Madame submitted a proposal for a Cape Auguet Eco-Trail in May 1998. If it is accepted, substantial improvements to the treadway, signage, and interpretive opportunities will be made in the coming years.

Further Information: Contact Development Isle Madame to access the background information compiled for their trail plan.

Cape George

Length: 4 km (2.5 mi) return
Time: 1 hr
Type: dirt road
Rating (1-5): 1

Uses: hiking, biking, horseback riding, ATVs
Facilities: none

Gov't Topo Map: St. Peter's 11 F/10
Trailhead GPS Reference: N 45° 44" 09.1', W 60° 49" 11.5'

Access Information: Turn off Highway 4 in the village on the paved road toward Oban, French Cove, and The Point, and follow it for 12 km (7.5 mi). Watch for a sign on your right for Bras d'Or Lighthouse Camp Ltd. Turn right, and follow the dirt road for 1 km (.5 mi). Continue past the turnoff to the campground and park your vehicle near the beach beyond. Follow the road on foot.

Introduction: Bras d'Or Lake is a 260 km² (100 mi²) somewhat salty body of water filling the centre of

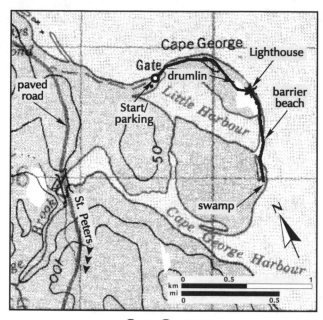

Cape George

Cape Breton Island. Because of its beauty, much of the coastline has been purchased for cottages, and more disappears from public access every year. Few opportunities exist to hike along the shore, but Cape George is a very short walk that permits anyone to spend a few minutes beside this famous body of water. From the lighthouse on the cape, all four counties on Cape Breton can be seen, and the distant hills of Benacadie, Briomachoal, and Cains Mountain will magnetically attract most of your attention.

The shores of Bras d'Or Lake have traditionally been an important region for the Mi'kmaq, and several of the largest reserves in the province can be found there, including Chapel Island, visible to the southeast from Cape George. European immigrants cleared large areas for farms and harvested the timber, but these have mostly regenerated. Because of its access to the sea, Bras d'Or Lake was once an area of significant commercial shipping, but more recently boating and sailing have become the principal activities on the lake. Since the 1970s, oyster, trout, and salmon aquaculture operations have been undertaken.

Trail Description: Park your car as soon as you reach the beach and follow the dirt road on foot. On your right are a number of trailers that serve as cottages and fishing shelters. Please do not disturb them. To your left you have a wonderful view into the centre of Bras d'Or Lake. On most days this is quite a windy spot, and the wave action then might make you think you are on exposed coastline. As you approach the distant end of the beach, about 300 m/yd further, you will notice a large pool of water on your right. This is Little Harbour, and your walk will take you to its far end and to the thin line of vegetation you can detect in the distance.

Once across the slender causeway separating Little Harbour from the lake, the road begins to climb up the small rounded headland of Cape George. This is a drumlin, a smooth hill formed from deposits of glacial till. Much of southern Cape Breton is covered by these distinctive land forms, and most of the islands near Cape George are partially submerged drumlins. Erosion of these glacial sediments has created the gravelly barrier beaches at both ends of Little Harbour. You can get an idea of how soft the drumlin soils are by the huge runnels etched into the roadway and its lake-facing slope.

After about 200 m/yd the road moves into forest, providing some protection from the wind. It is only a thin fringe of trees, however, and as you climb you will find some places, especially near the top, where you will want to walk into the trees on your left to get a better view. The vertical climb is only about 15 m (50 ft), and you have less than 500 m/yd of uphill walk before you begin to descend. As you emerge from the undergrowth into a large clearing, the trail splits. Continue straight, down the hill to the inviting red and white small wooden lighthouse.

You may choose to stop here and have some lunch. This is a wonderful place to rest and sightsee. Or you may continue following the old road as it drops down to lake level and onto cobble. The trail that separated earlier rejoins from your right. About 200 m/yd beyond the lighthouse, you reach the start of another thin barrier beach. You have reached the far end of Little Harbour, and, as you walk across this narrow treadway, on your right you will be able to spot the strand you crossed initially, often with waves breaking high over it. Watch for cormorants drying their wings in the calmer waters. Crossing the barrier beach is easy except during storms, and you will be able to distinguish the route favoured by ATVs in their passage.

At the far end of the slender barrier beach you reach an area of thick spruce growing on extremely wet and marshy ground. Although the ATV trail continues, it passes along the edge of a small pond through a bog where the water is almost waist-deep. Near the water's edge the cobble beach continues for about 100 m/yd, and there is a thin strip of relatively dry ground, but there is so much deadfall that it is very difficult to make further progress. You can push through and reconnect with the ATV trail after 150 m/yd of slow, unpleasant bushwhacking. If you do, you can follow that route around to Cape George Harbour and eventually back to the starting point. However, very rigorous effort will be required, and I do not recommend it. Instead, once you reach the deadfall, turn around and return to your car.

Cautionary Notes: Waves can break completely over the barrier beach at the mouth of Little Harbour during storms. Temperatures are much colder on the exposed beach and near the lighthouse when it is windy, which is often in spring and fall.

Hunting is permitted on this property. Starting in early October, hunting season varies from year to year and for different types of game. Contact the Nova Scotia Department of Natural Resources for detailed information before going into the woods. Wear orange for safety.

Cell Phone Coverage: Your cell phone will work well throughout the walk.

Capelin Cove

Length: 17 km (10.5 mi) return

Time: 4-6 hr

Type: barrier beach, coastal barrens, ATV track, dirt road

Rating (1-5): 4 (distance, rugged terrain)

Uses: hiking, biking, horseback riding, ATVs

Facilities: none

Gov't Topo Map: Framboise 11 F/9
Trailhead GPS Reference: N 45° 45" 14.1', W 60° 20" 38.3'

Access Information: From St. Peter's, drive 1 km (.5 mi) eastward the past canal and turn right onto Highway 247. Continue for 13 km (8 mi) until you reach Lower L'Ardoise, then turn left to follow the Fleur-de-Lis Trail. Drive approximately 40 km (25 mi) to the village of Framboise. Turn right onto Crooked Lake Road, and continue along the dirt surface. At the road junction after

Southeastern

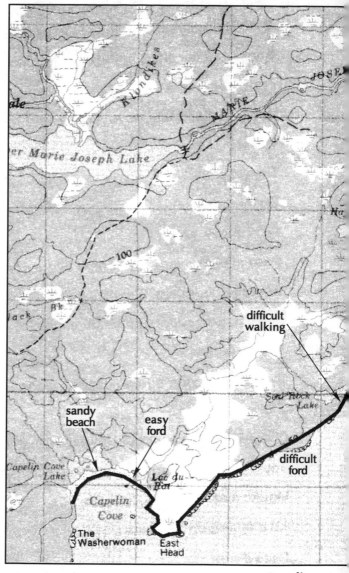

Capelin

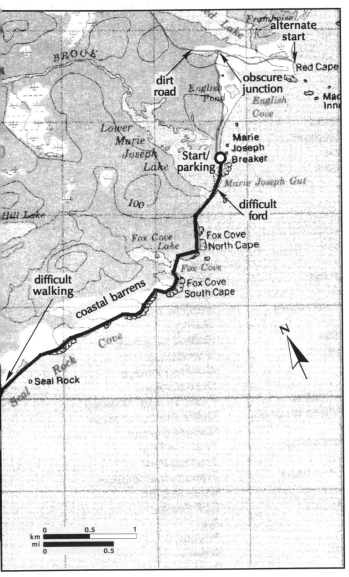

alternate
start

Red Cape

Mad
Inn

dirt
road

obscure
junction

English
Pond

English
Cove

BROOK

Lower
Marie
Joseph
Lake

Start/
parking

Marie
Joseph
Breaker

Marie Joseph Gut

difficult
ford

100

Hill Lake

Fox Cove
Lake

Fox Cove
North Cape

Fox Cove

difficult
walking

coastal barrens

Fox Cove
South Cape

N

Cove

Seal Rock

Seal Rock

| 0 | 0.5 | 1 |
km
mi
| 0 | | 0.5 |

Cove

1 km (.5 mi), keep left. At 3.3 km (2 mi), shortly after the road emerges from trees, look on your right for a very faint road, nearly grown over by alders. Crooked Lake should be visible on your left. You may choose to leave your car here and start your walk from this point, otherwise turn right and continue for 1.2 km (.75 mi) until the road ends near Lower Marie Joseph Lake.

Another option is to follow the Crooked Lake Road to its end on Morrisons Beach at Red Head and follow the coastline right from there. This adds almost 4 km (2.5 mi) to the total hiking distance.

Introduction: Anyone who loves beaches will enjoy this hike. From start to finish you will be following the coastline, crossing sand and cobble beaches created from the glacial till covering Richmond County in infinite variety by the relentless erosion of the pounding North Atlantic. Glaciers deposited layers of gravel and sand averaging more than 12 m (40 ft) thick over much of southern Cape Breton, with drumlins, large smooth hills of glacial till, being common. Red Head, the cliffs above English Cove to your left at the start, is an example of a drumlin almost completely consumed by the sea. The shoreline is indented with small protected bays, such as Capelin Cove and Fox Cove, and these nearly always shelter a sand beach.

I do not recommend this hike for children or novices. The crossing of Marie Joseph Gut can be very tricky and will require careful fording. For those who do walk it, however, I can promise that you will enjoy a wonderful trek through a marvellously attractive stretch of deserted coastline.

Trail Description: You cross a short cobble beach to Marie Joseph Gut, which you must ford. This outflow of the lake is very narrow; the water flows quickly, and it would be easy to lose your footing and be swept into the ocean, only a few metres away. Once across, put your shoes back on (and whatever other clothes you removed), and climb the drumlin, perhaps 15 m (50 ft) high, following the ATV track. The view here is magnificent, especially to the left into Framboise Cove. Your treadway is grassy and very easy walking, staying near the edge of the eroding cliff. At the second rise you enter an area of thick white spruce, then descend into Fox Cove, emerging from the trees onto its lovely sand and cobble beach, which holds back small Fox Cove Lake.

On the far side of Fox Cove the trail re-enters forest for a short distance while it climbs the small hill of South Cape. Your view when you leave the brush at the headland is breathtaking. The entire length of shallow Seal Rock Cove, more than 3 km (1.75 mi), is visible from where you stand. You can see the empty coastal barren where the next hour's worth of hiking will take place. Walking is extremely easy until you reach Seal Rock Lake at the next headland. Only occasional wet areas and short stretches which you must cross on rocky cobble slow your progress, and there is one small stream to hop over about 1 km (.5 mi) from South Cape.

Shortly before your reach the next pond, the ATV trail seems to end. The modest outflow from Seal Rock Lake is no obstacle, but the drumlin on the other side is thickly scattered with dead white spruce, virtually impenetrable. This forces you to cross about 500 m/yd of narrow, rocky beach below the cliff. During storms it would probably be unsafe. Exposed bedrock makes this section the roughest walking of the hike.

Fortunately, at the headland the ATV trail miraculously reappears, cutting across the top of the point and through spruce thickets. From here to East Head, at the mouth of Capelin Cove, your path is once again unconstrained. The ATV track is distinct, and after another 500 m/yd the trees on your right completely fade away, leaving you on a coastal barren more than 1 km (.5 mi) wide. As you approach East Head, the deep indentation of Capelin Cove will unfold on your right. Although a dirt road extends out to the coast and cuts off the headland, follow the shoreline instead and savour every second of your time at this special place.

The road leads into the interior and eventually, about 5 km (3 mi) further, it connects to the paved road, although far from any community. Follow the dirt road for a short distance where it runs next to the water, then turn off when you reach small Lac du Rat (Rat Lake) and start walking on the exquisite sandy beach. You must get your feet wet crossing the outflow of Capelin Cove Lake and Lac du Rat about 200 m/yd later, but you should have your boots off by then anyway! More than 1 km (.5 mi) of deserted beach is all that remains of this hike, although the ubiquitous ATV trail appears to continue into the woods at the far end of the beach.

Explore further if you wish, but I recommend that you spend some time relaxing in Capelin Cove before retracing your route back to Lower Marie Joseph Lake and your car.

Cautionary Notes: This hike passes through a completely unpopulated stretch of coastline; make certain you inform someone where you have gone and when you are expected back.

The outflow at Marie Joseph Gut can be very powerful. After a rain, the water will be waist-high or higher. I strongly suggest walking sticks or rope to assist in making the ford, and I do not recommend that a solitary hiker attempt it alone.

High winds constantly buffet this shoreline, making it substantially cooler than the interior, especially during storms and in spring and fall. For most of the hike you will have no shelter; dress warmly.

Cell Phone Coverage: There is no signal available at any point in the hike.

Delorier Island

Length: 9 km (5.5 mi) return
Time: 2-3 hr
Type: dirt road, beach
Rating (1-5): 2

Uses: hiking, horseback riding, ATVs
Facilities: none

Gov't Topo Map: Port Hawkesbury 11 F/11
Trailhead GPS Reference: N 45° 31" 52.1', W 61° 07" 42.8'

Access Information: Follow Highway 320 over the bridge onto Isle Madame. About 400 m/yd past the bridge, turn right and follow Highway 206 for about 6 km (3.75 mi) to the turnoff to Janvrin Island. Follow the paved road for almost 5 km (3 mi). Just after the one-lane bridge from Mussel Island crosses La Mouclière, the paved road turns 90° right. A dirt road turns left; park here.

Introduction: At approximately 1 cm (.5 in) per year, the coastline of Nova Scotia is sinking beneath the waters of the Atlantic Ocean. Chedabucto Bay, dividing this part of Cape Breton from the mainland, is a submerged river valley that has become a large arm of the ocean. Similarly, Le Blanc Harbour and West Arichat Harbour, separated by the long, thin breakwater of Delorier Island, would have been dry ground only a few thousand years ago. Much of Delorier Island is barrier

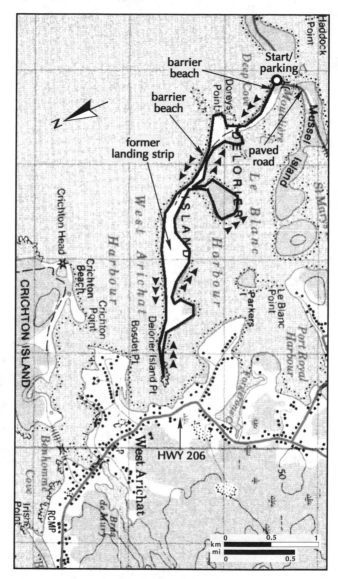

Delorier Island

beach, the reworked sediment of the sandstones, slates and shales that cover most of Isle Madame. Long barren cobble beaches connect small tree-covered hills that bulge into Le Blanc Harbour, their ocean-facing side having been eroded almost flat.

This walk is recommended for those who want a relatively easy coastal hike. Although it's not a maintained trail, footing is reasonably secure, there is very little elevation change, you have no vegetation to contend with, and the distance is within most people's capability. If you want to have a greater challenge each time you try a coastal hike, you could start with Delorier Island, follow it with the longer Point Michaud trail, work up to Capelin Cove, then attempt Cape Auguet, Lighthouse Point, and finally Gabarus – Belfry Gut.

Trail Description: At the start the dirt road is wide, deeply rutted, and very wet. A new house, built on the left about 100 m/yd in, has generated quite a bit of heavy traffic. If you wish, descend the hill by the parking area to the waterline and turn left. This works just as well. Once past the house, you rapidly move into a barren section and onto cobble beach. The road appears to continue, but it is probably only used by ATVs beyond this point. At the far end of the rocks, move to the oceanside and follow the coastline around rocky Doreys Point, which juts into the bay.

On the far side of this small headland, the coastline becomes another barrier beach connecting to the next wooded area. If you do not want to walk around the end of Doreys Point, you will find a distinct ATV trail at the end of the first beach that cuts through the forested centre of this little hill and arrives at the near end of the next beach. Crossing the barrier beaches is rather interesting; you have ocean on both sides, separated by only a few metres of rocky cobble, but the difference in appearance of the two bodies of water is substantial. The inland waters, on your left, are calm and shallow, and you can expect to see dozens of great blue herons deliberately stalking their meals in the shoals. The Chedabucto Bay waters, on your right, are active and often pound the beach, with rafts of eider and the occasional loon riding the swells.

Toward the end of the beach you reach a small area of red sand. This is all that remains of the near end of the drumlin in front of you, eroded away by the non-stop motion of the Atlantic. Follow the coast on the oceanside, weather permitting, picking your way among the large rocks that intrude from the sandy shore. As you can see from the hill rising on your left, erosion of the soft soils of these hills is very rapid.

As you follow the easy shoreline into West Arichat Harbour, there are many interesting sights across the water. Crichton Island, its small lighthouse at Crichton Head an obvious beacon, is about 1 km (.5 mi) to your right. This is another popular walking area, being connected to the village of West Arichat by a long, exposed breakwater. Directly ahead, the houses on Bosdet Point loom larger, and it appears that you will be able to walk right up to them. In fact, Doreys Island Point, the far end of the walk, is separated from West Arichat by barely 200 m/yd of water at low tide.

The beach gradually changes to become much rockier, with the sand portion mostly below the high-tide mark. Partway along the shore you will notice a distinct notch in the hill on your left. If you scramble up to the overgrown field beyond the crest, now covered in young beech and alders, you will be standing on the site of an emergency airfield used for anti-submarine patrols during World War II. Not much remains to be seen today, however.

Beyond this notch the hillside turns into a grassy

slope, climbs briefly up another small drumlin, then gradually lowers to beach level. The final 500 m/yd follow a long, thin spit of grassy land extending almost, but not quite, to the far shore. Houses are only a few hundred metres away on three sides, and traffic on busy Highway 206 passes just as close.

Now, however, you must return to your car, almost 4 km (2.5 mi) away. I suggest you walk back along Le Blanc Harbour, the interior coast of Delorier Island. The view here is quite different, with curving coastline that is not under constant attack from the same kind of wave action as on the other side. The hills are thickly vegetated, with only a narrow, sandy beach between trees and water. If you follow this shore all the way back to Doreys Point, you will add almost 2 km (1.25 mi) to the total distance.

Cautionary Notes: Most of this trail is along exposed beach. During storms, waves can be quite high, and that may necessitate walking on the inland side of the island only.

Cell Phone Coverage: Good coverage is available everywhere on Delorier Island. All phones should be able to make a connection and complete a call.

Further Information: *The Natural History of Nova Scotia*, Volume II, contains fascinating information about the Chedabucto Bay region. It is listed in District 860: Sedimentary Lowland.

Southeastern

Lennox Passage Provincial Park

Length: 4 km (2.5 mi) return
Time: 1-2 hr
Type: paved road, walking trails, dirt road, coastline
Rating (1-5): 1

Uses: hiking
Facilities: washrooms, water, tables, playground, beach

Gov't Topo Map: Port Hawkesbury 11 F/11
Trailhead GPS Reference: N 45° 35" 10.4', W 61° 01" 21.7'

Access Information: Follow Highway 320 over the bridge onto Isle Madame. Remain on Highway 320 until you reach the park, about 4.5 km (2.75 mi) beyond the bridge. The park entrance is on the left; for a longer hike leave your car near the gate.

Introduction: Lennox Passage Provincial Park is idyllically situated on the banks of Poulamon Bay on the north shore of Isle Madame. Although fairly small, 37 h (91 a), it boasts a walking trail that can combine with the road system for a pleasant weekend walk for young families and novice hikers. I particularly enjoy this walk during hunting season when the park is closed. It provides a safe haven for some outdoor exercise in the forest, and the grounds are lovely. This is a very busy park in the summer, when its beach, sheltered from the Atlantic winds, attracts many local residents, and the passage is crowded with recreational sailing vessels.

The first permanent settlement of Isle Madame occurred after the French lost most of Acadia, including mainland Nova Scotia, to the English in 1713, although it had been a summer base for European fishers since the time of Columbus. After the loss of Louisbourg in 1758

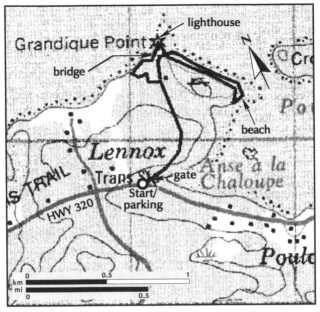

Lennox Passage Provincial Park

and the constant plundering by American privateers in the late 1770s, the population fell to six families. Afterward, many former families returned, seeking safe haven after decades of exile. Despite the difficulties of dishonest merchants, poor fisheries, and religious discrimination, these early Roman Catholic settlers instilled a fierce pride of place in their descendants. Today, Isle Madame has a population of more than 4000, mostly of Acadian descent.

Trail Description: From the park gates, follow the gravelled road through the mature mixed-wood forest toward the picnic area. Climbing gently initially, your route curves gradually left as it makes its way over a low, broad hill. After about 700 m/yd — by now you have started downhill — a small sign indicates the hiking trail, which heads into the trees on your left.

Wide and grassy, the footpath quickly passes through the fringe of hardwood near the road and into a superb area of white spruce reclaiming former farm fields. I find the uniform size of these trees somehow unnatural and intimidating, and the green mossy carpet with no underbrush surrounding the spruce looks as if it must be artificial, even though I have seen this pattern in dozens of other regrown areas. Now a carpet of needles, the trail soon reaches a ridge and junction. Directly ahead you get a glimpse of a large, very interesting-looking footbridge.

Turn left and follow the path, keeping left at all the next few junctions, as you skirt the park boundary, passing wild roses and old apple trees. You move out of the white spruce onto grass treadway and into a beautiful stand of poplars just before you reach the ocean edge of the shore at Lennox Passage. The trail turns right to parallel the coastline, emerging onto a grassy field in the middle of the picnic area. The bridge you spotted earlier is to your right, an elaborate structure high above a modest brook that does not even show on the topographical map. Cross over, taking a picture, and on the other side turn left and take the stairs back down to ocean level.

Grandique Point, with its unpretentious but charming red and white lighthouse, is directly ahead across the well-maintained lawn. From it, you obtain exceptional views of most of the length of Lennox Passage. The small community of Grandique Ferry, on the shore opposite, is the landing site of the small boat that connected Isle Madame to Cape Breton Island until 1928.

Leaving the point, head left uphill on the park road for perhaps 50 m/yd, where you will find a sign directing you into the woods to your left. A narrow, gravelled footpath plunges you into the thick, young trees, completely enclosing you in foliage. Not for long, however, for the trail constantly emerges from its sylvan passage to touch the edges of picnic sites and viewing stations. This path is ideal for children, winding in and out among the thick vegetation, providing good footing with no wet spots, and being barely wide enough for one to walk without brushing the trees on either side. Furthermore, if you feel you have walked far enough, you can leave the path any time by turning right and exit through a picnic site to the park road.

Some 600 m/yd further on, after passing a small connector path between the road and the ocean and walking through a more open area of softwood, you reach the end of the point on Poulamon Bay near Anse à la Chaloupe.

From here you have two choices. The signs direct you right to the park road, and right again to follow it back to the main activity area at Grandique Point. This can be very pleasant, especially in early June when young rabbits emerge to nibble on the new grass. I saw nine on my last visit. However, I prefer turning left, walking down to the beach shore, and turning left again to follow the coastline. Lennox Passage looks more like a lake than the ocean. There is usually very little wave action, and the tide range is barely 1 m (3 ft). Herons are very common in the shallow waters around here, and you might expect to sight various migrating seabird species. The walk is very easy, following the gently curving coastline back to Grandique Point, although you sometimes have to clamber over trees recently fallen from the eroding forest edge.

Once back at the lighthouse, follow the park road toward the flagpole and the large, wheelchair accessible washrooms. This is the route back to the park entrance; 850 m/yd remain in your hike.

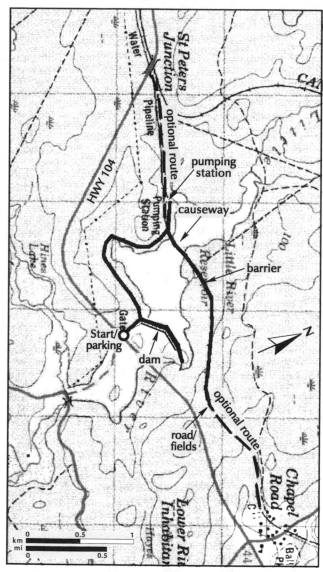

Little River Reservoir

Cautionary Notes: If you return to the lighthouse on the beach, there is some driftwood that must be climbed over. This part of the hike is not suitable for younger children or novices.

Cell Phone Coverage: Signals are very strong throughout, with no dead areas even in thick vegetation.

Little River Reservoir

Length: 9 km (5.5 mi) return

Time: 2-3 hr

Type: dirt road, abandoned rail line

Rating (1-5): 3

Uses: hiking, biking, cross-country skiing

Facilities: none

Gov't Topo Map: Port Hawkesbury 11 F/11
Trailhead GPS Reference: N 45° 36" 08.0', W 61° 15" 52.8'

Access Information: From Port Hawkesbury and Exit 43, the junction with Highway 4, drive 7.5 km (4.75 mi) on Highway 104 toward St. Peter's. Look on the left for a blue sign: Little River Pumping Station. Park near the gate completely off the pavement.

Introduction: During the 1960s and 1970s the lands around Point Tupper on the Strait of Canso were transformed into an industrial complex. Government policy was to concentrate and develop a heavy industry park in southern Cape Breton. An oil refinery, a massive paper mill, and a plant to create heavy water for use in nuclear reactors were all situated in a fairly small area near Port Hawkesbury. In addition to the construction of improved road, rail, and port facilities, large reservoirs of water had to be created for industrial use. Landrie Lake, still utilized today, was the closest source, but the Little River was also dammed and its water diverted by pipeline into Landrie Lake.

Some of the original industries, such as the infamous heavy water plant, have closed, and the demand for water is no longer as great as it was. The pipeline has been removed, as have the power lines to the pumping station, but the dam still remains. The road from the gate to the former pumping station is suitable walking for anybody and should constitute a pleasant Sunday stroll, especially in the fall. Adding the abandoned rail line turns this into a more demanding hike but one still suitable for average hikers.

Trail Description: Pass the gate and follow the wide, gravelled surface into the interior. Within sight of Highway 104 you encounter the junction with the route to the dam. For now, turn left and continue to follow the road. It is very easy walking, with few potholes and plenty of grass in the treadway, and it effortlessly conducts you around the western perimeter of the reservoir, although with a fringe of trees between you and the water. You reach the site of the former pumping station 2 km (1.25 mi) from the trailhead. This small rectangular structure sits just above an arm of the reservoir, and a few rusted remains of the former pipeline can be found to the left, in the direction of Point Tupper.

If you wish, you can follow the route of the water pipeline for slightly more than 1 km (.5 mi) past the pumping station until it reaches Highway 104 at St. Peters Junction, the spot where the Cape Breton Railway split from the mainline to travel to St. Peter's. Although the former rail line is completely overgrown, a clear path can be found under the power poles that once carried the wires providing electricity to the pumping station.

Otherwise turn around and walk back 400 m/yd to the first bend in the road. On your left you will see the lake, beyond a wide opening in the trees. You will also notice a gently curving earthen causeway connected to the far bank. This is the former rail line, bisecting the reservoir and providing a venue for excellent views of wildlife in the water. At its far end the route of the rail line is still distinct, although overgrown with alders. Nevertheless, I recommend you head into the growth and follow the grassy, dry treadway.

Within 100 m/yd the vegetation opens up slightly and very encouragingly, and you will find a sign warning of a barricade 500 ft (150 m) ahead. Because the rail line was elevated through here, it is dry and easy to follow, and I was surprised at the size of some of the trees growing in the middle of the bed. Just past the sign on your right is a small pond, which always seems to host some waterfowl. The metal barricade is still in place, but there is no evidence that anyone other than deer pass this way anymore.

The track stays moderately open until you reach another warning sign 150 m/yd beyond the barricade, then young alders grow thickly enough that you must work through them to pass. However, the treadway remains good, and I find a path like this more interesting than a wide open one. The former rail line continues to be easy to follow, becoming quite clear on hill slopes and dry areas, and with young trees crowding the centre in wetter spots. You pass within 150 m/yd of the eastern tip of the reservoir, but no path provides access. Continue for almost 1.5 km (1 mi), until you reach a large pit where soil has been removed. Beyond here the rail line has been converted into a vehicle road, and if you continue you will reach the community of Lower River Inhabitants in another 1.5 km (1 mi). To your right are a number of pasture fields, and Highway 104 is just be-

The gently curving former rail line bisects Little River Reservoir and provides an excellent place from which to view wildlife in the water.

yond the trees on their far side. If you do not wish to follow the old rail line back, you could return along the highway.

Once back to the reservoir road, turn left and follow it almost back to your car. At that first junction, within sight of the gate and where you originally turned left to walk to the pumping station, take the opposite fork and walk toward the dam. Through the woods for about 100 m/yd, this road leads to the long earthen embankment restraining the waters of the reservoir. Large stones cover the lake face of the dam, while the top and reverse slopes are covered in grass and, at the right time of year, flowers. Level and wide enough for two, the dam extends for 500 m/yd to a small hill. Walk over, and on the far side you will notice a small concrete barrier and the ruins of whatever facility originally regulated the outflow from the reservoir. Little River, constricted by the confined passage, cascades through a narrow, though not deep, gorge. This is a wonderful site to rest and have a bite to eat before you return to your car.

Cautionary Notes: There is no signage anywhere along this route. You may find the thick growth on some sections of the abandoned rail line disorienting.

Hunting is permitted on some parts of these lands, especially closer to Lower River Inhabitants.

Cell Phone Coverage: All phones should work at all locations in this walk, although weaker phones may have some difficulty in the very thickest vegetation. The signal is usually very strong.

Point Michaud Provincial Park

Length: 12 km (7.5 mi) return
time: 3-4 hr
Type: beach, ATV trails, rocky cobble
Rating (1-5): 2

Uses: hiking
Facilities: outhouses, picnic tables, beach, garbage cans

Gov't Topo Map: St. Peter's 11 F/10
Trailhead GPS Reference: N 45° 35" 32.0' W 60° 40" 47.5'

Access Information: From the St. Peters Canal, drive 1 km on Highway 4, then south on Highway 247 for 20 km (12.5 mi) toward Point Michaud (indicated on a road sign). The pavement ends approximately 1 km (.5 mi) past the Point Michaud Provincial Park entrance.

Introduction: Much of the land of Richmond County is low-lying, almost flat, with a highly eroded bedrock surface covered with glacial till, sands, and gravel. The exceptions are the hills bordering Bras d'Or Lake (Sporting Mountain and the East Bay Hills) and the Salmon River Lowland, the carboniferous sandstones around Loch

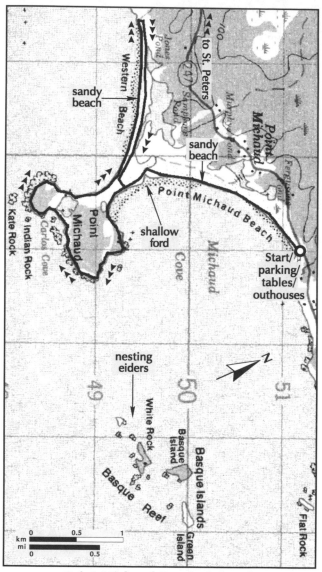

Point Michaud Provincial Park

Lomond, Lake Uist, and Enon Lake. This poorly drained area abounds with bogs, swamps, lakes, and slow-moving streams.

The rocky coastline, however, is dominated by large barrier beaches, very few of which ever receive many human visitors. Point Michaud Beach is at the southern end of the coastal till plain extending from Scatarie Island along the southeastern seaboard of Cape Breton Island. This coastline is relatively even and dips gently into the sea. Between Fourchu and Point Michaud there are extensive cobble barrier beaches enclosing large barachois ponds — ideal bird habitat. The relative re-moteness of the area seems to encourage a greater number of species to visit the marshes.

Point Michaud is one of Nova Scotia's best examples of a tombolo, a beach that has formed in the shelter of an island and then has connected that island to the mainland.

Trail Description: Starting in the parking lot of the picnic park, you begin at the eastern end of Point Michaud Beach. This gorgeous expanse of white sand stretches for more than 2 km (1.25 mi) in a gentle arc around Michaud Cove to the rocky promontory of Point Michaud. The beach is very broad and flat, and at low tide there is more than 20 m (65 ft) between the grass and the sea. This is gentle, effortless walking, with ample room be-tween the high tide mark and the vegetation.

About 1.5 km (1 mi) from the parking lot, a small brook drains into the ocean and interrupts your pro-gress. It is no substantial obstacle and can be easily forded, but it cannot be crossed without getting your feet wet. There is an extensive pond system behind the dunes of the beach; Murphys, Fergusons, James, and Sampsons ponds all drain through this one spot. Peeking over the dune tops, you may see several varieties of duck and shorebird in the ponds or among the marshy grasses.

Beyond the stream, a further 700 metres of sandy walk continues until the beach runs out and you start on the rocks of Point Michaud. An ATV track runs close by behind the dune system. As soon as you leave the sand you can begin following it. At first, it is wide and well-used, making for easy walking. Fishers have used Point Michaud for generations, and there used to be jetties at several locations on the headland. Now these have disappeared, and only faint traces of their presence remain.

As you start round the point, the Basque Islands can be seen directly ahead about two kilometres offshore. The sea in between is often filled with rafts of eider ducks riding on the swells. Stop and watch carefully, and sometimes you will discover that the seemingly empty sea is in fact populated by hundreds of these large, chunky ducks. They are also quite shy, so as you turn each corner of your walk, any eiders that sight you immediately head for the open ocean.

The path quickly narrows, and within another kilometre it almost disappears as you reach the stony ledges of the easternmost edge of the headland. The winds are always wild here and the temperature is quite a bit lower than on the sandy beach. As you continue round the point, you reach a little inlet, Carlos Cove, in the middle of Point Michaud. A tiny sandy beach with high cobble ledges separates the ocean from a surprisingly large pond. This is probably the prettiest spot on the walk.

On the far side of Carlos Cove, you turn another headland, and as you so do Isle Madame comes into view well toward the horizon to the southwest. Once round the point, the walking becomes much easier, with small grassy knolls climbing up as high as 8 m (26 ft) from the surf. This continues as you make the short remaining walk round Point Michaud and return to the pond at Carlos Cove, but now on its far side! Once again, only a narrow strip of land separates ocean and pond.

You are now at the head of Western Beach, which extends more than 3 km (1.75 mi) toward the small community of Gracieville. This beach is much narrower and steeper than Point Michaud Beach, and when you walk on it you cannot see beyond the top of the dunes. When you reach the end, at the bluish rocks near the houses, simply walk over the dunes and you will encounter an ATV track that runs parallel to the beach. Follow it back toward Point Michaud Beach. Make sure you have your binoculars ready, because the bird life in James and Sampsons Ponds is quite extensive, and you will have a good deal to observe.

As you near the base of Point Michaud, an ATV track connects the Western Beach to Point Michaud Beach — they are barely 100 metres apart. Once back on Point Michaud Beach, it is an easy 2 km (1.25 mi) walk back to your car at the picnic ground.

Cautionary Notes: Expect higher winds and lower temperatures on Point Michaud than inland, especially in spring and fall.

During storms, be cautious of approaching too close to the water's edge. This is open ocean, and rogue waves, several times larger than normal ones, can hit unexpectedly.

Cell Phone Coverage: There is strong coverage throughout the hike with no dead zones anywhere.

Future Plans: Point Michaud Beach is IBP (International Biological Programme) Proposed Ecological Site 26, a protected natural area where human influence is kept to a

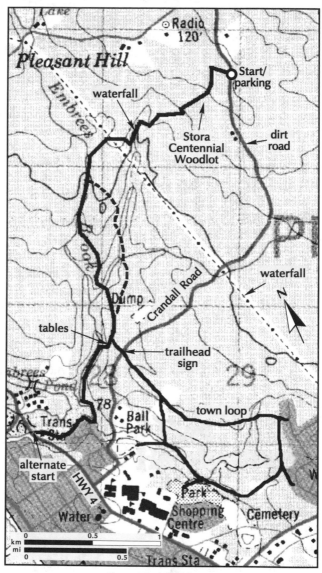

Port Hawkesbury

minimum in order to preserve characteristic or regionally rare ecosystems. Point Michaud is proposed because of its beach and sand dune system, which demonstrates the succession from bare sand to white spruce forest.

Port Hawkesbury

Length: 8 km (5 mi) return
Time: 2 hr
Type: footpaths
Rating (1-5): 2

Uses: hiking, cross-country skiing
Facilities: tables, benches, garbage cans

Gov't Topo Map: Port Hawkesbury 11 F/11
Trailhead GPS Reference: N 45° 38" 39.5' W 61° 20" 41.0'

Access Information: Enter Port Hawkesbury from Port Hastings on Highway 4. At the Toronto Dominion Bank, MacSween Street, turn left. Drive 100 m/yd, then turn left onto Crandall Drive. At the next stop sign, continue straight; Crandall Drive becomes Crandall Road. Follow the road for nearly 4 km (2.5 mi), keeping left at Artie Reynolds Road when the pavement ends. Watch on the left for the large trailhead sign of Centennial Woodland Trails.

Introduction: In order to salvage commercially valuable timber when the spruce budworm swept through Cape Breton forests in the late 1970s, vast areas were clear-cut. On the 54-h (133-a) Centennial Woodland property, wet areas and hardwood stands were protected, and greenbelts were established near small brooks; even so, 75% of the lot had to be cleared of dying trees. Experimental silviculture techniques were undertaken in the early 1980s, and approximately 10,000 indigenous and non-native seedlings were planted.

In 1989, as a hundredth anniversary present to the town of Port Hawkesbury, the Stora Enso forestry company constructed a network of walking and hiking trails in this area. With routes carefully designed to pass through plantations, greenbelts, and naturally reseeded areas, the trails show forest diversity and the lot's interesting features, including a small waterfall. The 2.4 km (1.5 mi) of walking paths and 5 km (3 mi) of hiking trails are open year-round. More recently, the Town of Port Hawkesbury has constructed community trails connecting various recreational sites and the Centennial Woodland Trails. These can be accessed from at least seven different locations, permitting walks of almost any distance you choose. Large signs displaying maps can be found at all major trailheads. Though always close to houses or a road on most of this system, you still enjoy the sense of being far back in the forest.

Trail Description: Pass the gate and walk down the broad gravel road to the sign displaying a map of the trail network. Interpretive panels can be found on all the walking trails, including this entrance lane. The route system on the woodlot is a maze, so any combination of paths can be put together for a walk. However, mazes can be somewhat confusing if you are new to an area. For example, the main trailhead sign is a junction for three broad walking paths. Fortunately, a nearby smaller sign reading Port Hawkesbury Community Trails points left; follow its advice.

Heading downhill on the broad, gravelled treadway for the 320 m/yd to the next intersection, you pass interpretive panels for balsam fir, red maple, and yellow birch, and you also get a good view of the Strait of Canso. Turn right, moving steadily downhill 180 m/yd to the next intersection past panels for red pine, jack pine, and Norway spruce. Turn left now, still heading downhill to the next intersection, 100 m/yd further, and turn right, following the arrows. Within 70 m/yd the gravel gives way to a narrow, natural-surface footpath, and you move into one of the old-growth greenbelts. From this point, watch for diamond-shaped orange route markers attached to trees 2 m (6 ft) from the ground.

The footpath follows a tiny stream over some little bridges and past two more well-signed junctions (keep left). After 250 m/yd it reaches the bank opposite a tiny but pretty waterfall, its water trickling in three staggered cascades over a slate outcropping. The woods here are very attractive, especially in summer when the rich green leaves of the many hardwoods form a protective canopy. Continuing on, the trail conducts you up the bank to a wide, clear-cut corridor underneath a power line. Visible on the far side is a large sign indicating the continuation of the Port Hawkesbury Community Trails outside the Stora Enso woodlot.

Beyond the power line, the trail heads directly to Embrees Brook. On the top of the steep eastern ridge, sometimes more than 5 m (15 ft) above the stream, the path works down the ravine through stands of hemlock and older hardwood. Rocky intrusions create small waterfalls, and at about 1 km (.5 mi), a large viewing platform has been built extending over the gorge and providing quite a view. This point is also a junction, one route continuing downstream and the other heading 90° left. Both are worthwhile choices, with helpful bridges and stairs and occasional benches for brief rests. They reconnect almost 1 km (.5 mi) later, shortly before the treadway once again becomes covered with fine gravel and white signs with blue arrows begin to indicate the route. In a few hundred metres you reach picnic tables, benches, and another trail junction. If you go left about 25 m/yd, you emerge from the woods on the Crandall Road beside a large trailhead sign showing a map.

From here you have several options. Following the trail across the road, you can complete a loop connecting several sports fields and the Strait Area Education and Recreation Centre (SAERC). Should you return to the junction near the picnic tables and take the other path, you descend quickly to Embrees Brook, proceed downstream to Embrees Pond, and end at the gazebo in Centennial Park on Highway 4. Or you can retrace your route back to the car, having completed about 6 km (3.75 mi).

The trip from the Centennial woodlot to Embrees Pond and back is 8 km (5 mi); hiking all the trails in the Port Hawkesbury system involves a walk of at least 13 km (8 mi).

Cautionary Notes: none.

Cell Phone Coverage: Coverage at almost all spots is very strong. In some of the deeper, narrow ravines, especially under thick vegetation, signal strength was lower, but calls could always be completed.

Future Plans: Port Hawkesbury intends to improve the existing trail network and possibly add additional connectors.

Further Information: Stora Enso Port Hawkesbury Ltd. provides a brochure about their Centennial Woodland Trails including a map of the complete network. To obtain a copy you may write to their main address or pick one up at: Stora Enso Port Hawkesbury Ltd., Woodlands Department, 609 Church Street, Port Hawkesbury.

Pringle Mountain

Length: 13.5 km (8.5 mi) return
Time: 4 hr
Type: former road, ATV trails
Rating (1-5): 3

Uses: hiking, mountain biking, cross-country skiing, horseback riding, snowmobiling, ATVs
Facilities: none

Gov't Topo Map: St. Peter's 11 F/10
Trailhead GPS Reference: N 45° 44" 57.1' W 60° 59" 09.6"

Access Information: Turn off Highway 4 in the village of St. Peter's on the paved road toward Oban, French Cove, and The Point, and follow it for 25 km (15.5 mi). Reaching The Point West Bay, look for the small un-named bridge crossing Pringle Brook. The entrance to the old road is 100 m/yd before the bridge, on the left between it and the MacLean residence. In 1998 the road was hidden by vegetation, but ask around; the people here are friendly and helpful. Park your car by the side of the road, making sure the wheels are off the pavement.

Introduction: The Point West Bay was first settled in 1851 by James Pringle. This explains why you will find Pringle Harbour, Pringle Brook, Pringle Island, Pringle Shoal, Pringle Mountain, and Pringle Lake in the immediate area. Alexander MacLeod (MacLeods Point, MacLeods Pond, MacLeods Hill, MacLeods Shoal, and MacLeods Brook) was the next recorded settler, granted land in 1857. This area had long been used by native peoples in their seasonal migrations; Indian Beach at the mouth of Pringle Brook is so named because it was the site of a regular encampment. The area prospered for a time, combining farming, forestry, and raising livestock, and in

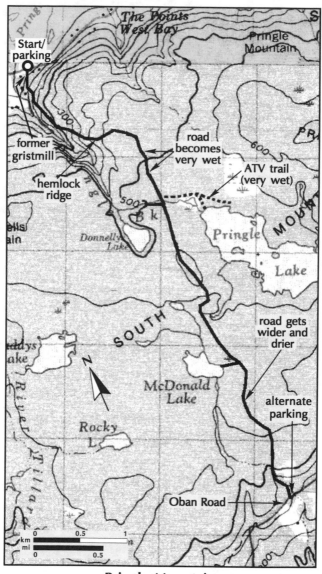

Pringle Mountain

1904 it possessed a carding mill, a sawmill, and a grist mill. But, like most of rural Nova Scotia, the 20th century has been a time of significant out-migration and population decline. Fewer live here now than in 1904, although you still meet people named Pringle and MacLeod.

Trail Description: Starting from the highway, the path leads immediately uphill. Providing clear walking under a softwood canopy, the trail, still a provincial road into the 1940s, runs past the ruins of the grist mill on the bank of Pringle Brook, scarcely 200 m/yd from the pavement. The mill was two floors high, constructed from hand-hewn stone, and some of the mill wheels remain inside. Please do not disturb anything. This is private property. You can examine the mill by turning right at a junction shortly after the start of the hike. Reaching a deserted house, walk behind it and locate the path to the mill. Its ruins lie next to a small cascade on Pringle Brook. Once, all this valley was cleared, the hillsides providing pasture for sheep. Retrace your steps to rejoin the main trail.

The path continues upward, quickly becoming rocky and rugged and climbing more than 150 m (500 ft) in the first 2 km (1.25 mi). Several areas resemble a creek bed, with deep washouts down the centre, although the treadway is fairly grassy. Houses visible across the ravine belong to local historian Will Pringle and other descendants of the original settlers. On your left, note and respect the No Trespassing sign. Turning away from the brook, the path begins to grow in, young beech and birch crowding the centre, although lovely old hemlock covers the steep hillside down to the creek below on your right.

When the trail levels out, it becomes significantly wetter, large puddles filling it from side to side. Indeed, this may be the wettest trail I have ever hiked, with one puddle almost waist-deep. The forest shows signs of logging and succession, with young spruce and pine growing in the shade provided by the older hardwood. The deep potholes filled with water are evidence that the road is used frequently without maintenance.

Reaching Pringle Brook, 2.5 km (1.5 mi) from the start, you have two options. You can turn left and follow the new ATV trail for 500 m/yd for a view of Pringle Lake, or you can cross over the bridge, turn right, and find a delightful spot for a picnic on a grassy knoll overlooking the brook. Although you will notice several fire pits, remember that this is private property. Do not camp without asking permission, and do not light a fire.

The trail is now much easier walking, suitable for two side by side (when it's dry, which is not often) with little elevation change. McDonald Lake is on your right through an area of open bog and clear-cut, an ATV trail running to another peaceful rest site on its shore. The path continues downhill another 2 km (1.25 mi) to the Oban Road, but it has been widened for logging and is not especially enjoyable except for the view of lower Richmond County. Return to The Point West Bay along the same route you hiked in.

Cautionary Notes: This trail is in a somewhat remote location, and you should let someone know when you are going in and when you can be expected back. There is no signage, so carry a map and compass. Also carry a secure source of water.

Hunting is permitted on these lands. Usually starting in early October, hunting season varies from year to year and for types of game. Contact the Nova Scotia Department of Natural Resources for detailed information before going into the woods. Although there is supposed to be no hunting on Sunday, always wear an orange garment for safety.

Cell Phone Coverage: All phones should be able to obtain a signal and complete a call anywhere on this trail except for the short section where the trail leaves Pringle Brook and curves behind the crest of Pringle Mountain. Even there, stronger phones might work.

Further Information: A brochure outlining 11 hikes and more than 90 km (55 mi) of walking opportunities in Richmond County is available at local tourist bureaus or by contacting the Richmond County Recreation Department.

St. Peter's Rail Trail – Battery Provincial Park

Length: 14 km (8.75 mi) return
Time: 3-4 hr
Type: walking paths, abandoned railway, road
Rating (1-5): 2

Uses: hiking, biking
Facilities: washrooms, tables, beach, camping, firewood

Gov't Topo Map: St. Peter's 11 F/10
Trailhead GPS Reference: N 45° 39′ 21.7′, W 60° 52″ 24.0′

Access Information: On Highway 4 in the village of St. Peter's, turn down Toulouse Street, in the direction of the Nicholas Denys Museum. Immediately behind the grocery store, on the right side, is the Bonnie Brae Senior Citizens Home. Park here; the trail starts at the far end of the building.

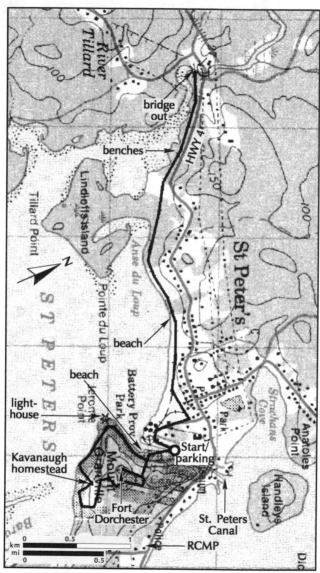

St. Peter's Rail Trail – Battery Provincial Park

Introduction: When the first train of the Cape Breton Railway made the trip from Point Tupper to St. Peter's in 1903, it was expected that this was only the first section of a line that would eventually extend to Louisbourg. The station in St. Peter's became home to the managing director of the railway and, when Canadian National Railways acquired it in 1921, the local agent. Few trains ran after the Lochaber Mines closed in the late 1950s, and when the line was abandoned in the 1970s, no one was surprised. Now some of it has come to life again as a walking trail along the banks of picturesque St. Peters Bay.

Used extensively by the Mi'kmaq as a portage, this narrow isthmus separating Bras d'Or Lake and the Atlantic Ocean was one of the first sites in the new world to be settled by Europeans: Portuguese in 1521, who called it San Pedro, French in 1650, who named it Saint Pierre. Both tried to take advantage of its convenient location. The former were driven away by cold, the latter by the English, who occupied Cape Breton Island in 1758. The canal, completed in 1869 after 15 years of desultory digging, handled large volumes of commercial traffic for many years. Today it is used primarily by pleasure craft.

Battery Provincial Park has 53 campsites, picnic grounds, and a beach on its 60-h (150-a) site. It also contains the remains of a British fort, on the heights of Mount Granville, and the ruins of the homestead of Lawrence Kavanaugh, the first English-speaking Roman Catholic to hold a legislative seat in the British Empire.

Trail Description: Wide and level, the former railway runs parallel to Highway 4 behind the houses on the main street. At the start, bushes have grown in quite thickly, but the treadway is still the grey-black cinders of the rail bed. A number of connecting paths enter from properties on both sides, showing considerable local use. The path heads down to the edge of St. Peters Bay, and once you pass the water filtration plant there are no more houses between you and the ocean. You can see Isle Madame in the distance, and often the bay is dotted with boats heading to or from the canal.

Open for most of the next kilometre, the path runs along the water's edge and also moves away from any houses. Properties are very large in St. Peter's, so the back lawns provide quite a buffer for the trail. You will pass several benches in this section, as well as signs warning that you are on crown land. As the trail follows the curving bay left, Lindloffs Island begins to dominate your view. Take time to leave the trail and explore one of the small beaches along here.

By the time the trail begins to curve right near Anse du Loup, ATV use is evident; some major wet spots must be avoided. Little roads begin to cross the trail now, and spruce close in, enfolding you as if you were much deeper in the forest. But within a kilometre Highway 4 approaches to within a few metres on your right and remains there for the rest of the hike. On your left, River Tillard also draws close, often visible through the trees. There are frequent connections with the road, and several more benches can be found in the last kilometre.

The end of the trail is clearly indicated by one final bench and a considerable amount of wood piled across the railbed. Beyond this point, the path is not maintained. River Tillard is only about 200 m/yd further. Turn around and retrace your route. You will have walked 7 km (4.25 mi).

The trails in Battery Provincial Park make an interesting addition to this walk. From the former railway station, walk down Toulouse Street to the mouth of the St. Peters Canal, about 500 m/yd. Turn left and follow the canal until you reach the locks, where you can cross to the other side. From here, the main interpretive site in the park is visible about 100 m/yd away.

A further 3 km (1.75 mi) of walking on very good paths is possible in the park if you visit the ruins of Fort Dorchester, the Acadian lime kiln site, and the Kavanaugh homestead ruins. Start from the interpretive panels at the mouth of the canal, and climb the hill to Fort Dorchester. The highest point near St. Peter's, it affords views of both the bay and the canal. Trails lead you through the camping area to the Kavanaugh homestead ruins down near the water. The path leads beneath a stand of lovely silver maple as it follows the coastline back to the park administration building and lighthouse and returns to the canal. Except for the climb up to Fort Dorchester, this is a very easy accompaniment to the abandoned rail line.

Cautionary Notes: At River Tillard, the bridge has been removed; be extremely cautious.

Cell Phone Coverage: An adequate to strong cell phone signal is available throughout the hike. The weakest signal is around River Tillard under forest cover; the strongest is at the top of Battery Park. There are no dead spots.

Further Information: A brochure about Battery Park printed by the Nova Scotia Department of Natural Resources is available from their Parks and Recreation Division.

Southeastern

Looking back toward Creignish Mountain from the Ceilidh
Coastal Trail near Long Point.

SOUTHWESTERN REGION

More than any other part of Cape Breton, the area of Inverness and Victoria counties below the Highlands make up the Gaelic heart of the Island. Creignish, Mabou, Glendyer, Dunvegan, Glencoe, and Lake Ainslie are communities whose very names echo with the lilt of the original homesteaders' Scottish history. The recent popularity in North America of Celtic music owes much to the musicians from this area. Ashley MacIsaac, the Rankin Family, and Natalie MacMaster are perhaps the best known, but they are only the latest of a proud heritage extending through many generations in these hills.

The land is divided between the Avalon Uplands and the Carboniferous Lowlands natural theme regions. At one time nearly all the lowland areas were farmed in small homesteads, and the hills were cleared for grazing sheep and cattle. Over the past hundred years the farms have been abandoned one by one as the young people move to the cities to find work, and the hillsides have grown over in thick succession forests. Myriad logging roads and old cart tracks wind through nearly every valley.

The paths of Strathlorne Forestry Complex are the only interpretive hikes, and Fraser's Trail will be a particularly pleasant experience for new hikers. The route along the coastal road from Dunvegan to Broad Cove Chapel, originally described in *Walk Cape Breton* (1975), provides easy access to a beautiful and rugged section of the western coastline. The trail in Whycocomagh Provincial Park, though short in distance, requires a challenging climb to reach its splendid lookoffs. Highland Hill, which also provides scenic viewpoints, is an interesting mixture of working woodlot and recreational pathways.

Perhaps the best hiking trail system in Nova Scotia, the marvellous network of the Mabou Highlands, can be sampled on either the Beinn Bhiorach trail, which is suitable for most walkers, or the Loop, which features much more vertical climb and is far more demanding. Marble Mountain and Pipers Glen – Egypt Falls both follow abandoned roads, the former the path of lost industry, the latter into a valley of forgotten farms. Two long linear trails, the Ceilidh Coastal Trail and the Mabou Rail Trail, follow the future route of the Trans Canada Trail.

Hunting is permitted in the areas of the Ceilidh Coastal Trail, the Highland Hill and Mabou Highlands trails, the Mabou Rail Trail, and the Marble Mountain and Pipers Glen – Egypt Falls trails. Hunting season usually starts around the first of October, but it varies from year to year and according to species. Contact the Nova Scotia Department of Natural Resources for detailed information before going into the woods. Although hunting is not permitted on Sundays, wear bright orange every day in season for safety's sake.

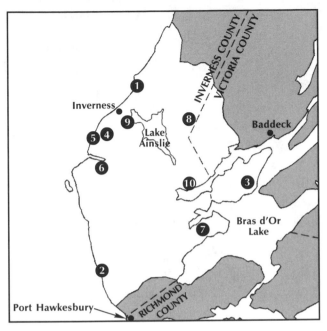

SOUTHWESTERN REGION

Southwestern

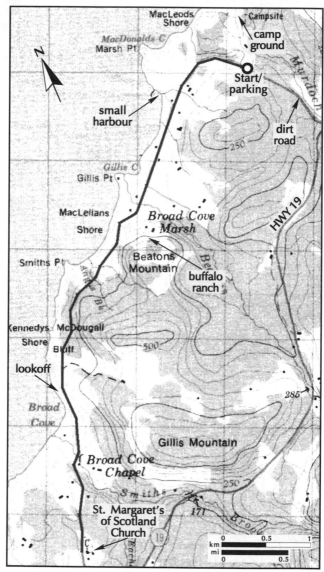

Broad Cove

Broad Cove

Length: 13.5 km (8.5 mi) return

Time: 3-4 hr

Type: dirt road

Rating (1-5): 2

Uses: hiking, biking, horseback riding, ATVs

Facilities: none

Gov't Topo Map: Margaree 11 K/6
Trailhead GPS Reference: N 46° 18" 12.0' W 61° 14" 32.2'

Access Information: From Inverness, drive 10.5 km (6.5 mi) north along Highway 19. Turn left at Dunvegan at the sign for Broad Cove Marsh. Continue down the dirt road for slightly more than 1 km (.5 mi). MacLeod's Campground is on the right down the hill. Park your car and start walking along the dirt road. If you have two cars, you can leave one at the end of the hike at St. Margaret's Church, Broad Cove Chapel.

Introduction: In 1809 Duncan MacLeod arrived from mainland Nova Scotia and began to work land near the mouth of Murdocks Brook. In 1832 he had his property formally granted to him by the government. Today the MacLeod family is still very much in evidence in the Inverness area, running campgrounds, cottages, and restaurants. The community of Dunvegan was originally known as Broad Cove Marsh, but had its name changed by charter in 1885 to commemorate the original village on the Island of Skye, Scotland.

Following a seldom-used dirt road, this route was listed in *Walk Cape Breton* as the Broad Cove Chapel – Marsh Point Trail, a coastal hiking trail for people uninterested in a rugged or tiring walk. Originally sceptical about hiking an active road, I changed my mind after a hike on a blustery September day. The walk through

Southwestern

Broad Cove Marsh was very pleasant, and the view south along the Inverness shore to the Mabou Highlands was splendid. Extending the trip to St. Margaret's Church adds hills and distance and makes this walk good exercise as well. I recommend this to anyone, especially those staying in the campground at Dunvegan. This trail is also a fantastic choice for a run.

Trail Description: At the start, the road is wide and gravelled. There is plenty of room to park your car without blocking traffic. You begin hiking on a low ridge above MacLeod's Campground, the western horizon a wide vista of the Gulf of St. Lawrence beyond the low hills, with a direct view of lonely Sea Wolf Island, a National Wildlife Area, 4 km (2.5 mi) off the coast.

Follow the road as it gradually descends toward sea level, turning left about 90° as it passes through an area of brush and young trees. A small hill, Marsh Point, rises between you and the ocean, diverting small streams to either side of it and creating a large, open marshy area on your right. Once past, you encounter the few weather-beaten houses still standing in Broad Cove Marsh, almost deserted by year-round residents. A few boats drawn up by the breakwater and traps along the shoreline indicate that some people still earn their living from this tiny harbour.

The road parallels the coastline now, quite close to the water. On your left, broad grassy fields that once were grazing land for sheep sweep up the sides of the low hills, while Beatons Mountain, directly ahead, still has animals roaming its steeper sides. These are not sheep, however. This is Blue Water Buffalo Ranch, and Donald Beaton is attempting to raise a herd of western bison in this little corner of Cape Breton.

Until the road crosses Beatons Brook and begins to climb the hill, at about 2.5 km (1.5 mi), it is wide and in very good condition except for a few places where the eroding coastline threatens it. Past the turnoff to Blue Water Buffalo Ranch, it narrows and gets much rougher. You leave the houses behind as the track climbs Beatons Mountain and enters an area of vegetation. This area, known as MacLellans Shore, has high sea cliffs which are sometimes quite close to the road. Be careful of the crumbling edges.

When you cross the bridge over tiny Angus Brook you will have walked about 3.5 km (2.25 mi), and afterward the road turns away from the water to pass behind Smiths Point. Moving through some thicker woods, you temporarily lose sight of the ocean. Then about 500 m/yd further on you sight Cape Mabou, rising ahead. Walking a further 500 m/yd downhill you find a lookoff obviously frequented by cars. Your view south is tremendous, but expect the wind to be much more brisk than previously. From Broad Cove to Sight Point, the coastline stretches out beneath you, with the imposing mass of the Mabou Highlands dominating the far skyline. The sea is always active along this coast, waves endlessly pounding the exposed shore and eroding the soft carboniferous soils around Inverness. The white gypsum cliffs of Plaster Rocks mark the far end of Broad Cove.

Heading downward again, the road bends left to follow the hill as it curls in to meet Smiths Brook. A few houses cling to the open southern face of Gillis Mountain, but the road remains narrow and rough until you cross the bridge over the brook. From here you turn inland, climbing by more houses and fields before the road levels out, shortly before you reach the paved road in front of St. Margaret's of Scotland Roman Catholic Church in Broad Cove Chapel. A cemetery fills the large field on your left. If you have time, explore it and find the names of the first Scottish settlers from the early 19th century.

Some people still earn a living from the tiny harbour at Broad Cove Marsh.

End your hike here. To return to your car (if you haven't left one here), either retrace your route or continue on the paved road for about 1 km (.5 mi) to Highway 19. Turn left, and follow the highway, which is very busy, especially in summer, back to Broad Cove Marsh Road. Distances of both routes back are about the same.

Cautionary Notes: This is a road, not a trail. Expect the occasional car.

There are high, sheer cliffs on eroding coastline over much of route. Stay back from the edges.

Cell Phone Coverage: A very weak signal is available though most of the walk, and I could not make a connection or complete a call. Frequent dead spots exist on low ground and whenever a hill interposes between the road and the ocean.

Ceilidh Coastal Trail

Length: 31 km (19.5 mi) return
Time: 8-12 hr
Type: abandoned rail line
Rating (1-5): 5 (distance)

Uses: hiking, biking, horseback riding, ATVs, snowmobiles
Facilities: water, outhouses, garbage cans, picnic tables, covered tables

Gov't Topo Map: Port Hawkesbury 11 F/11, Whycocomagh 11 F/14
Trailhead GPS Reference: N 45° 41" 42.2', W 61° 26" 38.0'

Access Information: From Port Hastings, drive 6 km (3.75 mi) on Highway 19 towards Port Hood. Turn left onto the dirt road at #1195, the first house on the left past Marg's Bed and Breakfast. Follow the road 500 m/ yd to where the former rail line crosses. Park there, but do not block the abandoned rail line. You can leave a second car at Long Point Provincial Park about 15 km (9.25 mi) further along Highway 19.

Introduction: On June 15, 1901, the railway from Port Hawkesbury to Inverness, operated by the Inverness and Richmond Railway Company, was opened for traffic. Purchased by Canadian National Railways in 1929, it continued to operate until the late 1980s, carrying coal from mines around Inverness to the main line at Port Hastings and the Canso Causeway. It was abandoned when the line's biggest customer, Evans Coal Mine, was shut down due to flooding.

Like so many of Nova Scotia's abandoned railways, with the removal of its tracks this former transportation corridor overnight became a broad recreational path. In 1995, the provincial government instituted an official policy reserving all its abandoned rail lines for use as

Southwestern

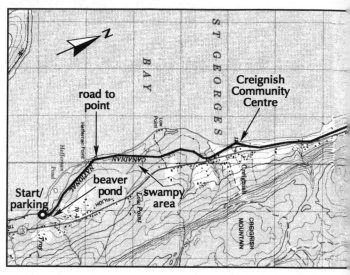

Ceilidh

trails, and in 1997 it obtained this section from Canadian National.

Even before its abandonment, the line bordering St. Georges Bay was a favourite of walkers because it follows the coastline for much of its length. Spectacular views make this one of the most scenic hikes in *Hiking Trails of Cape Breton*. Bikers and ATV users also use this pathway extensively. In 1997 and 1998, considerable improvements, particularly brush clearing and culvert replacement, were made by a local community trail-building association. Expect further development, such as signage and parking areas, in the next few years.

Trail Description: Although not signed, the trail is un-mistakable, wide and surfaced with small gravel. As you head north, Heffernan Pond, a significant salt marsh protected behind a thin barrier beach, becomes visible to

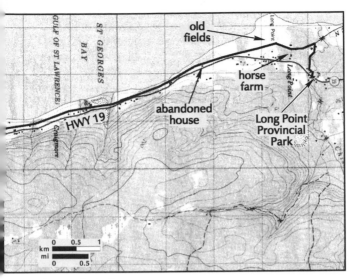

Coastal Trail

your left. As you cross a small trestle bridge, to your right is a freshwater pond swollen behind a massive beaver dam. Dozens of species of bird can be observed from the raised rail bed separating the two bodies of water.

Just the other side of the marsh, a fence and field lie on your right, and the trail enters the forest as a long straightaway begins. Numerous side paths enter the route from both directions, but it is not until about 1.5 km (1 mi) further on that a major dirt road crosses the trail. For a slight diversion turn left; Doogies Road reaches the beach at Heffernan Point in 50 m/yd. Beyond the junction, the trees on the coast side of the trail begin to thin, revealing Cape George on the far horizon and Low Point directly ahead. Turning the next corner, you encounter 100 m/yd where the treadway required substantial excavation and widening. Industrious beavers, damming small culverts under the railbed, flooded a large tract on the right, and portions of the trail were washed away. For much of the next kilometre drowned trees and swamp dominate the area beside the path.

In young forest again, the trail cuts behind Low Point on perfect treadway. At about 3.5 km (2.25 mi), you pass an old section house on your left, almost overgrown now, and at 4.0 km (2.5 mi), you reach the community of Creignish. Extensive repair works are frequent for the next kilometre as the trail runs behind homes and the community centre. Highway 19 is only 25 m/yd away, and numerous roads connect it with the rail line, which emerges into an area of broad fields. Creignish Mountain towers above the beautiful white church, the centre of the village.

Beyond Creignish, the treadway becomes rougher, with more roots and with brush growing on the path. Once across the long open area, the trail almost intersects Highway 19 opposite house #PH-015 before it moves into more vegetation. Nearby houses are common, and one resident has even placed a swing set on the railbed! Just past there, you encounter your first severely wet area, where a creek empties into the treadway at 7.5 km (4.75 mi).

The trail continues, frequently passing houses and driveways and staying close to Highway 19. Tremendous views of St. Georges Bay are common, the ocean slope falling quite steeply to your left and providing a broad range of vision when the trail passes fields. At 11 km (6.75 mi), an abandoned house on your right sits in the worst wet area. Expect soggy toes until the trail association repairs the drainage there.

Entirely grassy now, the trail continues straight for the next 3 km (1.75 mi), although the coast gradually bears left toward Long Point. About 600 m/yd beyond the deserted ruin, a picnic table in a well-maintained

Following the coast for most of its length, the Ceilidh Coastal Trail was a favourite of walkers even before the rail line was abandoned.

field provides a wonderful spot to stop and look back down the coast toward Creignish. The land near Long Point begins to flatten, the Creignish Hills (the Big Ridge) retreating inland. Follow the trail as it leaves both highway and coastline and passes through an area of tall larch, emerging into another area of former pasture land. The dunes of Long Point can be seen on your left, nearly 1 km (.5 mi) away. You cross another small trestle bridge, and soon the trail begins to curve right, entering forest once more.

You pass several more fields and farms, including a large barn complex on your left and a fenced field often containing horses on your right. When you pass the wrecked school bus, #71 Inverness District, about 600 m/yd of abandoned rail line remains. Skirt the wet area, pass another road 100 m/yd later, and continue until you reach the next dirt road crossing the track. If you continue to the large bridge crossing the brook, you have gone too far. Turn right, and follow the road as it cuts between an abandoned farmhouse and field, reaching Highway 19 and Long Point Provincial Park about 800 m/yd later. Rest awhile beside Chisholm Brook, then return the way you came. (unless, of course, you've left a car here).

Cautionary Notes: The bridges have no railings and only minimal decking.

ATV use is heavy, and although most users are courteous and reduce speed when approaching walkers, underage drivers are less predictable.

Cell Phone Coverage: Coverage is reasonably good throughout, stronger at the start of the hike. Near Long Point weaker phones may not be able to make a connection.

Future Plans: The abandoned rail line from Port Hastings to Inverness, nearly 90 km (55 mi), has been designated as part of the route of the Trans Canada Trail. Expect substantial improvements to bridging, signage, and access points over the next few years.

Highland Hill

Length: 7.5 km (4.75 mi) return
Time: 2-3 hr
Type: dirt roads, logging roads, former roads
Rating (1-5): 2

Uses: hiking, mountain biking, cross-country skiing
Facilities: interpretive panel, garbage cans

Gov't Topo Map: Grand Narrows 11 F/15
Trailhead GPS Reference: N 45° 58" 18.5' W 60° 52" 47.3'

Access Information: From Highway 105, take Exit 6 east of Whycocomagh toward Little Narrows. A short ferry ride crosses St. Patricks Channel where you turn right and follow Highway 223 toward Iona and Grand Narrows. Drive approximately 15 km (9.25 mi) until you reach McKinnons Harbour. A road sign advises that a skiing trail is within 3 km (1.75 mi) and directs you left up the unpaved Barra Glen Road. At the Highland Hill Road, another sign directs you left again; the trail is only 1 km (.5 mi) away. Continue uphill past Maxie MacNeil's house (#623) and sawmill. Keep right at the next junction; just past it on your left is a large parking lot and an interpretive panel.

Coming from the direction of Sydney, follow Highway 223 to Iona. A further 5 km (3 mi) takes you to Jamesville West and the sign warning you of the upcoming right turn onto the Barra Glen Road.

Introduction: Highland Hill is unusual because the trails are primarily on private land and in the middle of working woods. They begin and end on a 106-ha (262-a) property belonging to Maxie MacNeil, named Nova Scotia's Woodlot Owner of the Year in 1994 for integrating educational and recreational opportunities with his forestry uses.

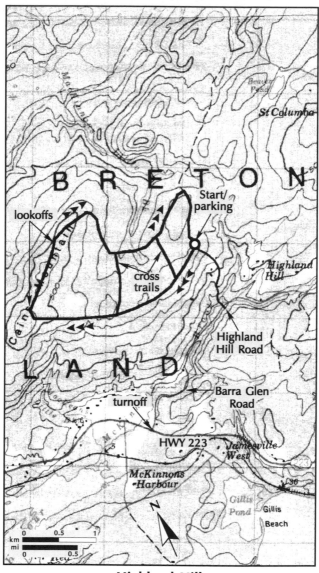

Highland Hill

An interpretive sign at the end of the parking lot explains the work going on in these woods today and the history of settlement and logging activity in this area. Nine kilometres (5.5 mi) of trails pass through 570 ha (1400 a) of upland forest that sustain forestry practices involving shelter wood, weeding, planting, and thinning. These lands were clear-cut in the 1920s and devastated by spruce budworm in the 1970s; there are no presettlement trees remaining, and you will observe contemporary, integrated resource management silviculture.

Established and maintained by the Clan Nordic Ski Club, the trails are used for both mountain bike and ski races, and are open for a range of recreational and educational activities.

Trail Description: Start on the left road, numbered Route 1 and named Peadair Custie's Trail. This is a wide, open wood road, as are most of these trails. You will soon notice a number of small yellow signs; these describe what forestry practice is being used on that particular patch of woods, the species involved, and the date of the work. After 300 m/yd you reach the first junction, with Route 5 on your right. The trail system is arranged as a stacked loop, with a small initial circular path having a second loop added to it, and a third loop added on to the second. Your hike can be 2.5 km (1.5 mi), 4 km (2.5 mi), or 7.5 km (4.75 mi) depending upon your fitness level or interest. The total network includes 9 km (5.5 mi) of trails.

To complete the full loop, continue straight. Shortly afterward, you will come upon a clearing on your left that has been put aside for Rankin Memorial School's commemorative tree plantation. Each year since 1994 the graduating class plants a block of a different species of tree. Little more than 1 km (.5 mi) from the start is the turnoff right for Route 3. Just past there is a section where new trees are growing up through the stumps of budworm-killed trees, providing an arresting contrast. Former homestead sites can be identified by the presence of old apple trees.

Crossing a small brook after about 2 km (1.25 mi), you begin your ascent of Cains Mountain. You are now on Route 2, and you can see all four counties of Cape Breton from its scenic lookouts. The directions are not signed, but you can easily determine where each is. Except for a large planted area of Norway spruce, the woods through which you walk are now mostly sugar maple and yellow birch. Recent thinning makes this section of trail extremely difficult, especially in the summer.

You may notice other wood roads, but your trail is marked with yellow rectangular symbols nailed onto trees. You may also notice a fair amount of wildlife. I scared up numbers of grouse as well as a very annoyed red-tailed hawk, and deer tracks were everywhere, particularly near MacKinnons Little Brook. Two eroding bridges cross the brook, and just after the second, as you climb the steep hill, the turn to Route 4 is almost hidden on your left. You have travelled more than 5 km (3 mi) and about 2 km (1.25 mi) remain no matter which path you select.

Route 4 is only 500 m/yd long and is named Bottom's Up. Maybe that is because it immediately descends to a small creek, then climbs the other side to the next junction. Route 6, Rabbit Run, on your left, takes you to Maxie's Road through the only very wet section in this system. A number of tiny log bridges cross seasonal streams. A planted area of white pine and fir provides warning that you have almost reached the road. Turn right to return to the parking lot, less than a kilometre away.

Cautionary Notes: Hunting is permitted on these lands with permission. Starting in early October, hunting season varies from year to year and for different types of game. Contact the Nova Scotia Department of Natural Resources for detailed information before going into the woods. Wear orange for safety.

There are no water or washroom facilities.

Little effort is made to maintain the trails for hikers. In summer, the vegetation nearly hides the trails and signage is minimal. They are easier to follow in spring and fall.

Cell Phone Coverage: There is a very strong signal on every part of the trail.

Further Information: The growers' association has produced an attractive free full-colour brochure of the trail that can be obtained from the Route 223 Co-op and local tourist centres.

An excellent reference to accompany this walk is *Trees of Nova Scotia: A Guide to Native and Exotic Species* by Gary L. Saunders. It can be ordered from the Government Bookstore in Halifax.

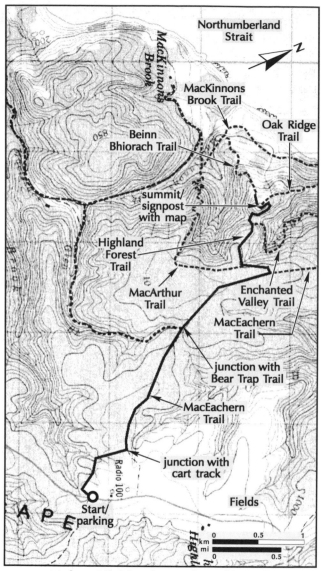

Northumberland Strait

MacKinnons Brook Trail

Oak Ridge Trail

Beinn Bhiorach Trail

summit/ signpost with map

Highland Forest Trail

MacArthur Trail

Enchanted Valley Trail

MacEachern Trail

junction with Bear Trap Trail

MacEachern Trail

junction with cart track

Radio 100¹

Fields

Start/ parking

A P E

0   0.5   1
km
mi
0   0.5

Mabou Highlands – Beinn Bhiorach

Mabou Highlands – Beinn Bhiorach

Length: 10.5 km
   (6.5 mi) return
time: 3 hr
Type: old cart tracks,
   walking paths
Rating (1-5): 3

Uses: hiking
Facilities: none

Gov't Topo Map: Lake Ainslie 11 K/3
Trailhead GPS Reference: N 46° 08" 59.8' W 61° 22" 54.0'

Access Information: From Inverness, drive south 14 km (8.75 mi) on Highway 19 to the road to Glenora Falls. Turn right and follow the dirt road, much of it steeply uphill, 5 km (3 mi) to the junction with North Highlands Road 600 (snowmobile sign). Turn right and drive for 3 km (1.75 mi). The Cape Mabou trailhead is on the left, just before a large area of fields. A small parking area is available.

Introduction: The Mabou Highlands form a rounded knoll 15 km (9.5 mi) long by 8 km (5 mi) wide, reaching an elevation of 335 m (1100 ft) at the north end and 320 m (1050 ft) at the south. Formed of highly erosion-resistant, metamorphosed sedimentary and volcanic rocks, the surface is highly dissected and the sides deeply eroded. Many trails in the Mabou Highlands are quite challenging, requiring strenuous climbs to reach the best viewing sites. However, for those who might not be comfortable hiking steep hills, it is still possible to reach the Beinn Bhiorach lookoff on a substantially level path. I selected this route, made up of parts of the MacEachern and the Highland Forest (Coill à Bhraighe) trails, starting from the Cape Mabou trailhead, to permit people to reach this magnificent view without too much stress on their knees.

Southwestern

The MacEachern Trail is named in honour of Allen J. MacEachern, Deputy Prime Minister of Canada, 1977-1984, and Senate Leader until his retirement in 1996; his family homestead and birthplace are near the trail-head at Sight Point. The former cart track links the coast with the South Highlands community pasture, still used today, atop Cape Mabou.

Trail Description: The Cape Mabou entrance is not as well used as those at Sight Point and Mabou Post Road, and in the summer vegetation nearly hides both path and parking area from detection. The trail immediately enters the woods, crossing over a small brook on a substantial footbridge. For the next kilometre, the indistinct footpath winds through the forest, skirting wet areas and frequent deadfalls. Watch closely for flagging tape; this will help keep you from wandering off the narrow track.

When you reach the former cart track, turn left, and you will note an immediate improvement in conditions. Two can walk abreast now, and the treadway is much firmer. The trail passes through thick stands of white spruce, providing abundant cover overhead. The blue paint splotches you notice on some trees date from earlier trail-building efforts in the 1980s. You are walking on the plateau on the top of the highlands through here, so no scenic view is available in any direction yet.

Your path leads gently downhill, and when the trees change to predominantly hardwood you know you have nearly reached the junction with the Bear Trap (Trap à Mhathain) Trail, 2.4 km (1.5 mi) from the start. Continue straight; the trail climbs a few hundred metres, then levels out until you reach the junction with the Highland Forest Trail 1.2 km (.75 mi) later; the sign may say Beinn Bhiorach Trail. From here, leave the Mac-Eachern Trail, turning left onto a footpath that curves around the top of the narrow gorge that contains the Enchanted Valley Trail far below. For the first time on your hike, you begin to get views of the ocean and the surrounding hills. About 300 m/yd along the Highland Forest Trail, the MacArthur Trail links up on the left. Continue to follow the curving path, as the slope on your right becomes increasingly steep. Soon you reach a broad ridge populated exclusively by hardwood that offers beautiful open walking. Watch for orange markers on the trees, however, because ferns grow so thickly here that they obscure the trail.

At the end of the ridge, the trail switches back to descend into a softwood-forested col where the Enchanted Valley (Gleann Sidh) Trail separates on the right to work its way down the ravine to the MacKinnons Brook Trail. Enticing though this appears, continue past it, and climb the remaining few hundred meters up to the summit of Beinn Bhiorach. (The sign at the Enchanted Valley Trail junction says only 200 m/yd remain when you begin your climb, but it seemed more like 400 m/yd to me.)

The reward, however, is more than worth the effort. You emerge from the trees onto a broad, open, grassy area with a stunning view of the Northumberland Strait. Look carefully, because on a clear day you can see Prince Edward Island on the western horizon. A large trailhead sign marks the junction of the several paths that access this lookoff, and its map reveals several optional return routes that you might consider if you feel particularly energetic. Before you leave, take time to explore a few metres along each of the Oak Ridge (Rids An Daraich) and Steep Mountain trails. Both provide different and excellent views of the slopes and valleys of the western edge of the Mabou Highlands. When you are ready, return along your original route.

Southwestern

Cautionary Notes: Hunting is permitted on these lands. Spanning early October to mid-February, hunting season varies from year to year and for types of game. Contact the Nova Scotia Department of Natural Resources before going into the woods. Wear orange for safety.

Cell Phone Coverage: No calling is possible from the MacEachern Trail, but the signal strength increases as you approach the ocean. Once you reach Beinn Bhiorach, you can telephone your friends and tell them what they are missing.

Future Plans: Continuing improvement of the existing network is planned over the next several years, including benches and several new trails.

Further Information: An excellent and informative brochure printed in 1998, *Hiking Trails of the Cape Mabou Highlands*, is available for $2 at local stores or by mail (include a stamped self-addressed envelope) from Cape Mabou Trail Club, Inverness NS B0E 1N0.

Mabou Highlands Loop

Length: 16 km (10 miles) return
time: 6 hr
Type: old cart tracks, walking paths, dirt roads
Rating (1-5): 5 (distance, rugged terrain, steepness)

Uses: hiking
Facilities: none

Gov't Topo Map: Lake Ainslie 11 K/3
Trailhead GPS Reference: N 46° 08" 30.9' W 61° 26" 47.8'

Access Information: From Canso Causeway drive north on Highway 19 to Mabou. In town, turn left on an un-numbered paved road toward Mabou Harbour. Drive 5 km (3 mi), turning right on the dirt road to MacDonalds Glen. Continue 7 km (4.5 mi) to the bridge at Mill Brook just past the last house and clearing. Drive up the small hill on the other side and look for the large trailhead sign on the left. Park here, not blocking the road.

Introduction: The Mabou Highlands, once the home of many industrious Scottish immigrants, now lie mostly deserted, save only for a few cottages. The former roads connecting their farms have become a network of challenging and exciting trails, courtesy of the Cape Mabou Trail Club. In 1998, twelve different trails totalling more than 30 km (18.75 mi) of maintained paths were available. For this hike I have combined portions of five of the trails into a loop that should pleasantly occupy a full day.

Trail Description: This walk starts at the base of Cross Mountain, so named because of the large Christian cross erected on its barren summit in memory of a 19th-century fishing tragedy. A large sign, displaying a map of

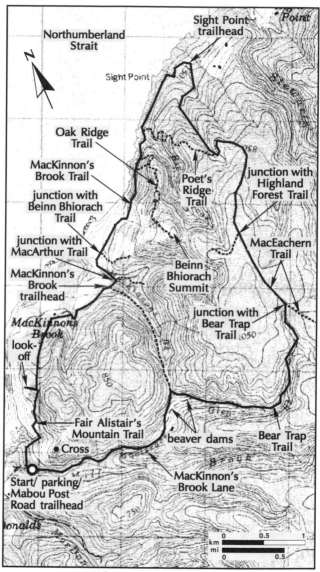

Mabou Highlands Loop

the entire trail network, directs you left up the open slope heading toward the ocean. Turning into a shallow ravine, crossing a tiny brook, and swinging onto an open rocky slope, the well-defined path climbs Beinn Alasdair Bhain (Fair Alasdair's Mountain). Near the summit a short side-trail to your left provides a wonderful vista looking south that you must not miss; Findley Point, Mabou Mines, and MacDonalds Glen lie beneath this very steep hillside. Continuing north, the main trail follows the route of an old road through dense white spruce, which is reclaiming former farmlands. Note the many piles of stones and the old fences. Unmarked side-trails can guide the adventurous to stone foundations, but there are no signs, so be cautious. At the base of Beinn Alasdair Bhain, the trail joins a dirt road at a metal gate, and the road becomes your trail for 500 m/yd until reaching the MacKinnons Brook trailhead, a major trail junction.

Turn left off the road into the woods and descend briefly to cross the brook. This is a lovely spot to camp. The trail turns sharply left and follows the curve of the hill toward the ocean. As you near the water, spruce gives way to spacious meadows. In July, these fields come alive with fireflies. Turning right again to parallel the coast, the trail climbs continuously as the hillside becomes steeper. Entrances to both the Beinn Bhiorach and the MacArthur trails branch to your right in the kilometre between MacKinnons Brook and a sign warning you of the hazards ahead. Climbing to nearly 150 m (500 ft) above the water, the path becomes less than 1 m (3.25 ft) wide, hugging the cliff above a straight drop to the ocean. There are even ropes for assistance at some of the most difficult spots.

After crossing Big Brook, where the Oak Ridge Trail connects on your right, the path becomes easier over the last kilometre to the Sight Point trailhead, where you will find another trail map posted. The new Enchanted Valley and Poet's Ridge trails also branch off to your right between Oak Ridge and Sight Point. At the Sight Point trailhead, turn right and walk inland along a dirt road until it crosses a creek. The MacEachern Trail follows the gully left and upward on the toughest climb you will face. Following the creek initially, then crossing the top of the plateau, this trail climbs to 320 m (1050 ft) in 3 km (1.75 mi).

This is a lovely walk, in late May a green and white carpet of Dutchman's breeches. At 1.2 km (.75 mi) from the Sight Point trailhead, you encounter the well-signed junction with the Poet's Ridge Trail. This is a good place to rest after your steep climb, then continue straight on. Very shortly afterwards, the path turns sharply left and leaves the brook, climbing the final elevation in a long, curving route. Reaching the plateau, the climb; is far more gradual and walking is much less laboured. You reach the junction with the Highland Forest Trail, which the sign may call the Beinn Bhiorach Trail near the summit 2.8 km (1.75 mi) from Sight Point. Continue straight, following the grassy track until you reach the junction with the Bear Trap Trail, 4 km (2.5 mi) from the Sight Point trailhead and less than 500 m/yd after the trail starts downhill.

Turn right; follow the Bear Trap Trail as it parallels the increasingly steep fall of MacIsaacs Glen Brook. A wonderful but always very wet 3-km (1.75-mi) stroll down a curving, steep-sided ravine follows, ending at the dirt road that is MacKinnon's Brook Lane. To return to your car, turn left and continue downhill on the road a further 2 km (1.25 mi). Look for a series of impressive beaver dams creating large pools on both sides of the road near the first bridge crossing.

Cautionary Notes: The path on the sheer 150-m (500-ft) cliff at Sight Point is very narrow with no railing, and at one point a rope assists you in scrambling over a particularly rough spot. Small children and pets should not be taken through here, nor should anyone disoriented by heights attempt this part of the route.

Hunting is permitted on these lands.

Cell Phone Coverage: Coverage varies in quality but is generally available at higher elevations when facing the Northumberland Strait. No calling is possible in ravines, under thick foliage, and on most inland sections of the trail.

Future Plans: Continuing improvement of the existing network is planned over the next several years and includes several new trails. Consideration is being given to a link with the Trans Canada Trail.

Further Information: An excellent and informative brochure printed in 1998, *Hiking Trails of the Cape Mabou Highlands*, is available for $2 at local stores or by mail (include a stamped self-addressed envelope) from Cape Mabou Trail Club, Inverness NS B0E 1N0.

Mabou Rail Trail

Length: 24 km (15 mi) return

Time: 6-7 hr

Type: abandoned rail line

Rating (1-5): 4 (distance)

Uses: hiking, biking, horseback riding, ATVs

Facilities: none

Gov't Topo Map: Lake Ainslie 11 K/3

Trailhead GPS Reference: N 46° 01" 22.5' W 61° 27" 13.8'

Access Information: From Port Hastings, drive 51 km (30.75 mi) north on Highway 19. The trailhead is at Southwest Mabou on the left before the road crosses the Southwest Mabou River, where the former railroad intersects the highway. Look for the large clearing on the left and park there. It might be convenient to leave a second car further along Highway 19 at Mabou Station or on Highway 252 at Glendyer Station.

Introduction: This is one of the most attractive inland sections of abandoned rail line in Nova Scotia. The view of the Mabou Highlands from the Southwest Mabou River is stunning, and the stretch alongside the Mabou River to Glendyer Station is a paradise for birders. Although I have profiled this as one long hike, you can start at Mabou Station and head east to Glendyer Station, 9 km (5.5 mi) return, or in the other direction to Southwest Mabou, 17 km (10.5 mi) return. This walk is suitable for anybody who is comfortable with the distance.

Trail Description: Your route immediately heads through a deep cut in a ridge, then down and across a new embankment which replaces a destroyed bridge over Delhanty Brook. On the far side, vehicle paths lead left up the hill and right to the farm buildings below. Once across the gully, you will not notice any further elevation changes for the remainder of the hike, and the treadway becomes dry, flat black slag with lots of grass, wide enough for two to walk side-by-side. For the first kilometre, you walk north paralleling the river, which is below to your right. The forest is fairly thick through this section, and the slope on your left is quite steep.

The Campbell Brook bridge crosses high above the alders lining the banks below. It has no railings or decking; you should be extremely careful with your footing and maintain a firm grip on compass, binoculars, or anything that could drop. On the other side, the trail gradually curves right to avoid the hill rising steeply across your path, and the river closes in until it flows adjacent to the treadway. Note the many large dead trees lining the river banks. Eagle and red-tailed hawk frequent this stream all summer and fall.

Squeezed between river and hillside, the railbed is eroded by the many small streams that flood down the steep slopes; at about 2.5 km (1.5 mi), a washout sign warns snowmobilers of one particularly serious site. At 3 km (1.75 mi), the rail line crosses the river over a high metal bridge and skirts a coal-black hill, while the river veers sharply left. A few hundred metres later, a large pond appears on your right, then a cleared field. Crossing a little brook at the far end, the rail line curves left to clear another small hill. You will notice now that the hills are becoming smaller, the trees are almost entirely hardwood, and there is evidence of clearing on the tops of the hills on the opposite bank.

Becoming visible directly ahead, the Mabou Highlands fill the entire horizon and create a dramatic backdrop to the river estuary. The Southwest Mabou River expands rapidly as it approaches Mabou Harbour, creating a broad marshland several hundred metres wide and teeming

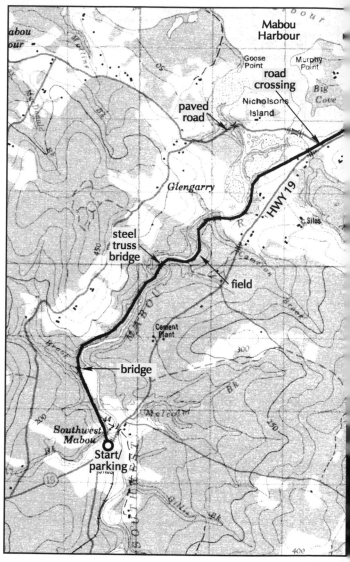

Mabou

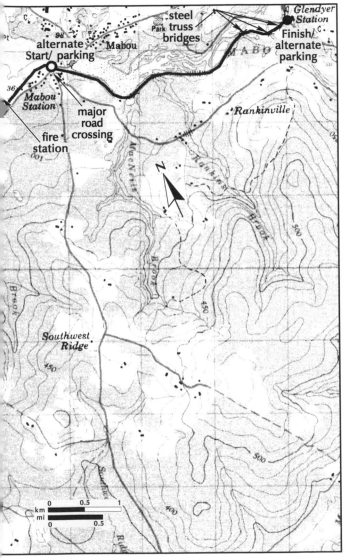

steel truss bridges

Glendyer Station

Finish/ alternate parking

alternate Start/ parking

98

Mabou

Park

M A B O U

Mabou Station

36

major road crossing

Rankinville

fire station

100

N

MacNeils

Rankin

Brook

Brook

500

Brook

450

450

Southwest Ridge

450

500

0   0.5   1
km
mi
0   0.5

400

Southwest

Ridge

Rail Trail

with bird life. Cameron Brook, at 4 km (2.5 mi), necessitates crossing another small, undecked railway-tie bridge, and for the next kilometre the river flows immediately beside your path on the left. Then the rail line turns away from the river into a long straightaway passing through an area of young, thick hardwoods that restrict viewing substantially. On your right, fields have been cleared almost to the old railbed, and large potholes filled with water, evidence of heavy ATV use, become frequent.

Highway 19 is visible on your right, moving closer as the rail line emerges from the brush to cross first an embankment over Allan Brook, then the road to West Mabou Harbour, at about 6 km (3.75 mi). Side by side, road and trail head into Mabou Station, the rail line dodging behind the volunteer fire station and most of the houses of the community. Just before the line reaches the Mabou River and turns right, a crossing to a new home on the left, built up quite high, cuts across the route.

You must cross the highway, and you do so near the entrance to the Mabou River Hostel and Suites before the road bridges the Mabou River. The trail enters a dense section of hardwood for the next 500 m/yd; the village of Mabou is visible through the leaves on your left. When you emerge from the trees, between the river and the small pond draining MacNeils Brook, the view of Mabou Village, its white church steeple rising out of the trees, is magnificent. You cross another railway trestle bridge here, and one more a few hundred metres further on at Rankins Brook.

Now the trail closely borders the broad and meandering Mabou River, with marshy areas perfect for ducks on both sides of the rail line. Study the high dead trees out in the marshy areas. If you do not see at least one bald eagle, you have not looked closely enough. For the next

3.5 km (2.25 mi), your attention will probably be entirely focused on the river and the broad marshy grasslands of its flood plain.

When you reach a steel truss bridge, you are nearly at Glendyer Station. Continue another 250 m/yd, and you encounter a second of these large structures. Neither has railings, but both have limited decking that provides easier footing. After a further 100 m/yd you reach a paved road, Highway 252. To return, either re-trace your route or turn left and follow the road to Mabou, then left on Highway 19 to Southwest Mabou.

Cautionary Notes: Bridges on the trail have no railings, only minimal decking, and often cross fast-moving rivers.

You must cross Highway 19 at Mabou Station. The road is usually busy, and drivers' visibility is limited because of vegetation and the curving road.

Cell Phone Coverage: There is no coverage anywhere on the hike.

Future Plans: The entire abandoned rail line from Port Hastings to Inverness has been designated as the route of the Trans Canada Trail. Expect substantial improvements to bridging, signage, and access points over the next few years.

Southwestern

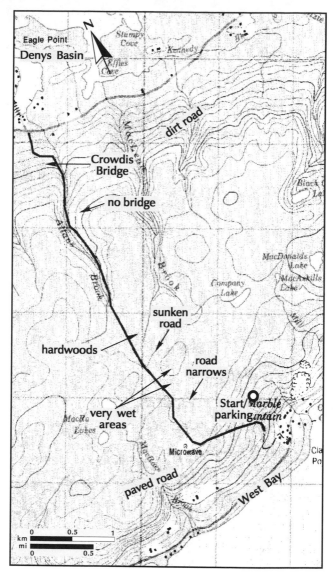

Eagle Point
Denys Basin
Stumpy Cove
Effies Cove
Kennedy
dirt road
Crowdis Bridge
no bridge
Black La
MacDonalds Lake
MacAskills Lake
Company Lake
sunken road
hardwoods
road narrows
very wet areas
Start/parking
Marble untain
MacRae Lakes
Microwave
paved road
West Bay
Cla Po
km   0   0.5   1
mi   0   0.5

Marble Mountain

Marble Mountain

Length: 11.5 km
  (7.25 mi) return
time: 3-4 hr
Type: gravel road,
  former road, bog
Rating (1-5): 3

Uses: hiking, mountain
  biking, cross-country
  skiing
Facilities: none

Gov't Topo Map: Whycocomagh 11 F/14
Trailhead GPS Reference: N 45° 49" 20.5' W 61° 02" 43.7'

Access Information: From Highway 105, take Exit 4 at Iron Mines toward Orangedale. As you reach Orangedale, watch for the sign for Crowdis Bridge and Marble Mountain. Turn right just before the village; if you cross the train tracks, you have gone too far. At Crowdis Bridge turn left onto a dirt road that becomes paved after 3 km (1.75 mi). About 19 km (11.75 mi) after Crowdis Bridge you reach the community of Marble Mountain. Look for the Mountain Road sign. Turn right between two churches and drive 2 km (1.25 mi) on a dirt road to a parking area just past the last house, #84 Mountain Road.

Introduction: In 1868, a visiting geologist accidentally discovered a seam of marble worth commercial exploitation. By 1900, the quarry employed more than 750 men, and the community housed more than 1000 people. Marble Mountain thrived, with several churches and stores and a busy port, as barges transported the gleaming white blocks to far markets. But the site was soon exhausted; the mines closed, and the community gradually disappeared. The remains of the quarry, a huge white hole chewed out of the hillside, are an unmistakable landmark for boaters and anyone driving on the opposite shore of West Bay

Southwestern

A pleasant walk is available around the old quarry grounds and along the shore. The beach in Clarke Cove is quite large and covered with white marble sand. Bring your bathing suit. On the road, more than 15 m (50 ft) above the water, there is an attractive lookoff with a few picnic tables, a good spot to eat lunch.

Except for the steep climb at the start and the general sogginess, this is an enjoyable hike and should be reasonable for even the moderately experienced. However, in 1975, *Walk Cape Breton* ended the hike at the top of the hill by the microwave towers and described the old road as difficult walking. This route will appeal to hikers, not walkers.

Trail Description: The road beyond the parking area is still used for a further kilometre, but only by four-wheel drive vehicles. Almost all your climb, approximately 200 m (650 ft), is completed in the first 1.5 km (1 mi). But your reward for this exertion is an ever-improving view of West Bay and its many small islands. In summer the lake will be dotted with recreational sailing boats, and Marble Mountain is a popular anchoring place. Almost at the summit, the road splits. To the left, perhaps 100 m/yd away, is a large microwave tower, and a gravelled surface leads there. The old road plunges into the forest directly ahead and immediately narrows to an overgrown cart track.

The trail nearly levels off, having reached the plateau area, and almost immediately it gets soggy and boggy. Whenever it's not wet, however, the treadway is pleasant and grassy. Dead spruce lie everywhere, remains of the spruce budworm infestation of the 1970s. The next kilometre is extremely wet, a creek bed in places, and sometimes I was knee-deep in water. Alders almost choke the path in some places, and you may wonder if it is worth continuing. After perhaps 800 m/yd, you reach a large bog through which the road was built. The roadbed has disappeared, sunk back into the fen, and the path is visible only because of the rows of small larch and the bushes that outline both sides. You can also see the clearing for the road in the trees on the far side.

Across the bog, the vegetation changes, and hardwood becomes much more common. Some of the maple is quite old, and as you climb again on drier treadway seas of small ferns replace the grasses. When I was there, the only disturbance though these plants was a single deer path. There is only this small hill to climb, and then the trail begins the long, gradual descent toward the other side of the mountain.

When you cross a small corduroy bridge in fairly good condition, you have reached the halfway point. For most of the final 3 km (2 mi), the trail follows Allans Brook down the hillside as it grows from a tiny trickle into a deepening gorge. Again the treadway gets very wet, with thick grasses growing waist-high in the summer. Little deadfall obstructs your route, and the woods open up on either side to permit views of the hardwood slopes. Allans Brook sounds very loud in these quiet surroundings, gathering strength with every metre as the thin soils of the steep hills drain into it.

At 4.5 km (2.75 mi), the trail crosses the brook, but this time there is no bridge. You must ford, and in some weather the flow can be surprisingly powerful. Traverse slowly and carefully. Now on your right, Allans Brook loses altitude rapidly while the path clings to the drier slope. Footing improves considerably, especially when the track is 5-10 m (15-30 ft) above the water. When the path turns distinctly left, away from the stream, you have less than 1 km (.5 mi) of trail remaining. Soon the Creignish Hills become visible on the horizon. Trees become younger and thicker, narrowing the trail. When you reach a junction, turn right. Within 250 m/yd you emerge on the highway at Crowdis Bridge, with the volunteer fire department perhaps 200 m/yd to your right. To return to your car, retrace your steps.

Cautionary Notes: The former road, while quite distinct to experienced hikers, has been abandoned for decades and is substantially overgrown. There is no signage, so I do not recommend this hike to beginners. This walk is extremely wet, even in summer.

Hunting is carried on in these lands.

Cell Phone Coverage: Coverage is adequate near both Crowdis Bridge and Marble Mountain. Signal strength weakens on the higher plateau, and some phones may not work. In the ravine descending into Crowdis Bridge no signal can be obtained.

Further Information: There is a small museum open in the summer months with photographs and artefacts from Marble Mountain's heyday.

Pipers Glen – Egypt Falls

Length: 14 km (8.75 mi)
return
Time: 3 hr
Type: dirt road, footpath
Rating (1-5): 4
(steepness)

Uses: hiking, biking,
horseback riding,
ATVs, snowmobiles
Facilities: none

Gov't Topo Map: Lake Ainslie 11 K/3
Trailhead GPS Reference: N 46° 11" 46.4' W61° 07" 27.2'

Access Information: Leave Highway 105 at Exit 5 in Whycocomagh and turn onto Highway 395. Continue on Highway 395 along the shore of Lake Ainslie and beyond Scotsville to Upper Margaree and the junction with the road to Egypt Brook and Keppoch, 31 km (19.25 mi) from Whycocomagh. Turn right and follow the dirt road for 2 km (1.25 mi) to the junction with the Pipers Glen Road. Turn right, crossing the bridge over Egypt Brook. Follow the narrow dirt road for 1 km (.5 mi), mostly uphill. When the road turns left and starts to descend, watch carefully on your right for a white signpost with red lettering that says Egypt Falls. Park on the road but do not block the thoroughfare.

Introduction: Like so many now-deserted valleys in Cape Breton, busy farms once lined the hills rising from Matheson Glen Brook. The original settlers, around 1843, were Roy McLennan from Eigg, Scotland, Hugh Stewart from Moidart, and Lauchlin Jamison from the isle of Canna. Pipers Glen received its name to mark the prowess of Lauchlin's son, Neil Jamison, who earned local fame for his piping.

Egypt Falls, one of the most attractive waterfalls on Cape Breton, is one of the more difficult to visit. Al-

Southwestern

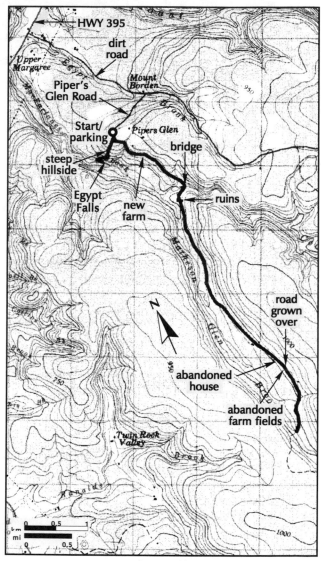

Pipers Glen

though the path from the road is scarcely more than 500 m/yd long, the descent is about 120 m (400 ft), some of it nearly vertical and requiring assistance from ropes tied to trees. The return climb will be an effort for even the very fit. I do not recommend this for young children or people who have any health concern.

The road through Pipers Glen was active until a few years ago, and it even shows as paved on some maps. However, beyond Cooper Brook only one farm remains, and grass is starting to cover the treadway. This is an easy, pleasant walk through a valley that skirts the southern fringe of Gairloch Mountain, the southernmost section of the Highlands Terrestrial theme region. Although I have recommended turning around when you reach Matheson Glen Brook, the old road can be followed to Middle River, more than 20 km (12.5 mi) beyond Gairloch and Gillanders mountains.

Trail Description: The route to Egypt Falls is straightforward. A distinct path leads downhill from the road, and some trees are marked with red flashes. The hardwoods on this steep slope are quite lovely, although you may have more time to appreciate them on the return climb. Very quickly you reach the cliff overlooking the river, where the path heads right, picking its way down the difficult hill face. Ropes have been strung to provide assistance, but there are no other constructions on this route. Once you reach bottom, turn left, and you arrive at the bottom of this unusual waterfall, wider than it is tall. In Cape Breton, rivers normally cut narrow, deep channels into highly erosion-resistant rocks. At Egypt Falls, the water has washed away the much softer Horton group rocks of the Carboniferous period to expose some of the tougher Fisset group basalts.

Climb back uphill to your car, then start striding downhill along the Pipers Glen Road. You could easily drive another 4.5 km (2.75 mi), but the dirt road is good walking and there is no traffic, so why not proceed on foot? You will find a small sawmill on your left 200 m/yd downhill. Until you reach the bridge over Cooper Brook, the route is quite wide and open. Passing a barn and newly cleared fields on your right, you get a clear view of the valley below. The road curls tightly around the hillsides near Cooper Brook, passing old fields and the ruins of farms. Horses are sometimes pastured in these fields, behind an electrified fence, and they are quite friendly to anyone offering apples.

Past the ruins, the woods close in somewhat, and the centreline grows over with grass. For the next 3 km (1.75 mi), the old road leads further up the valley, frequently passing large abandoned fields. Most of the old buildings have collapsed and are piles of rubble, but nearly 4 km (2.5 mi) in, one house remains relatively intact, with tattered fragments of curtains still in most of the windows. Nearby open fields, often containing old apple trees and with broad views of the valley in both directions, provide unlimited opportunities for wonderful camping, with permission. Your treadway is completely grass now, the remains of stone fences lining either side.

About 400 m/yd beyond the deserted house, the road re-enters the woods. On your left, you will notice a small cabin with bars over the windows (against bears), a new chimney, and an outhouse. It is still used as a hunting camp. The final 1 km (.5 mi) descends steadily but is choked by alders and deadfall, especially the last section beyond a small brook. I recommend you go no further than Matheson Glen Brook. To help identify it, the path on the far side climbs quite steeply, heading west. Retrace your steps to return to your car.

Cautionary Notes: Hunting is permitted on these lands. There is no signage and no traffic once you pass Egypt

Egypt Falls.

Falls. Notify someone of where you are hiking and when you expect to return.

Most of the land in the valley is private property. The crown right-of-way is restricted to very little space on either side of the road. Please do not damage either vegetation or artefacts.

Near the base of Egypt Falls ropes are provided to help you descend the steep slope. Footing is extremely poor and often slippery.

Cell Phone Coverage: No signal can be obtained anywhere on this hike.

Future Plans: Pipers Glen is IBP (International Biological Programme) Proposed Ecological Site 13, a natural area protected to preserve characteristic or regionally rare ecosystems. This area was nominated because of its spectacular waterfall and mature mixed forest.

Further Information: Egypt Falls can be found in both *Waterfalls of Nova Scotia* and *Explore Cape Breton*.

Southwestern

Strathlorne Forestry Complex

Length: 4 km (2.5 mi) return
time: 1 hr
Type: walking paths
Rating (1-5): 1

Uses: hiking, cross-country skiing, snowshoeing
Facilities: picnic tables, benches

Gov't Topo Map: Lake Ainslie 11 K/3
Trailhead GPS Reference: N 46° 11" 34.7' W 61° 17" 52.7'

Access Information: From Inverness, follow Highway 19 approximately 5 km (3 mi) southward. A small sign on the west side of the road indicates hiking and skiing trails. Turn off Highway 19 and follow the dirt road straight through a four-way junction 400 m/yd down the MacIsaac Road. Watch for the sign, at about 900 m/yd, and turn right to end in a parking area with a large interpretive panel.

Introduction: The Strathlorne Forestry Complex, established in 1978, is the largest forest nursery in the province. Occupying the original Fraser Grant of the 1800s, the objective of the nursery has been to provide trees to replace the forest devastated by the spruce budworm infestation of the early 1970s, when virtually the entire forest cover of large areas of Cape Breton was wiped out.

Established in 1993, these trails are designed not only for recreation but for education as well. Passing through stands of forest being treated using various silvicultural techniques, the route follows a brook and passes by an active beaver dam. The complex has developed a number of educational programs in wildlife and forestry management that they offer to elementary schools in

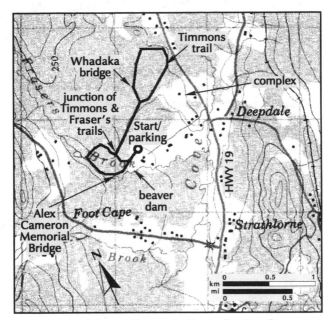

Strathlorne Forestry Complex Trails

the area. More than 1000 students a year pass through the complex.

This is a good introductory walk for people who are unaccustomed to hiking or who wish to learn more about Nova Scotia's woodlands. Short, mostly level, and well signed, this walk should be possible for almost all fitness levels. Note, however, that these paths are not wheelchair accessible. The two trails profiled, Fraser's and Timmons, are each loops linked by an 800 m/yd connector path.

Trail Description: Check out the large display panel before you start your walk. It contains a map of the trail system, and just to its left is a small round sign that tells you of the wetness situation on each of the trails and what footwear is recommended. Follow its advice unless you want to return with soggy sneakers.

The hike begins to your left at the far end of the parking lot. A path of wood chips defines your route across a small field, and at the vegetation boundary you will find a sign that says Entrance. You cross a little bridge and find a trail junction, where you turn left, following the Fraser's and MacDougall trails. Immediately on your left is a small pond created by beavers when they built their dam. It is home to an active colony, so watch for signs of their activity in the trees nearby.

The trail, except for a small detour over a rise between stations 2 and 5, quite closely follows a small brook for the next few hundred metres. Several of the trees along it are signed, enabling you to distinguish many of the common native species. Just past station 8, you will notice flagging tape to your left, and about 25 m/yd further along the trail, you reach the junction with the MacDougall Trail. The flagging tape marks the cutline used by cross-country skiers in winter to access the MacDougall Trail, but do not try to hike there. At the junction, a sign directs you over the little Alex Cameron Memorial Bridge, where you will find a map of the trail system and a notice saying that the rest of the way is under construction and not suitable for hikers.

Recross the bridge and continue left along Fraser's Trail. Station 10 immediately precedes the Snake Bridge, unrailed corduroy over a small wet area. Fraser's Trail is an excellent footpath, mostly surfaced in wood chips and wide enough for side-by-side walking. The section along the brook is very tranquil, and the frequent signage will be reassuring to novices.

After station 11, the trail leaves the brook and turns uphill. Passing through areas of thinning and strip cutting, you return to a junction with the Timmons Trail behind the tree holding area. Turn left and follow the path as it skirts the back of this area, crosses a dirt road, and continues along a wide, at times grassy, track. When you encounter a long section of corduroy, about 800 m/yd along, you have reached the base of the loop. Continue straight, following the direction indicated by the blue arrow.

The path now passes through woods where considerable thinning has taken place, and several of the trees here are identified by species. A short clear-cut interrupts, and signed metal posts conduct you across it and onto a wood chip treadway. You cross the Whadaka Bridge, where you come upon a display of dwarf mistletoe and witch's broom set slightly off the main path.

After nearly a kilometre, you emerge from the trees onto a large grassy field close to Highway 19. A cross-country ski sign with an arrow points to your right, and you will notice a row of metal posts extending across the field toward the south. Follow these. As you hike in the open, the main building of the complex is on your left. Coming down off a little rise, the route parallels a row of softwood until it returns to the forest. A map-sign shows that you have nearly completed the loop; continue past some trembling aspen, over a tiny bridge, by choke-cherry and white birch, and onto the large corduroy boardwalk.

When you come to the junction, turn left and return to the junction with Fraser's Trail. Turn left there, and walk about 100 m/yd downhill to the parking area.

Cautionary Notes: none.

Cell Phone Coverage: There is no coverage available anywhere on this hike.

Future Plans: The nursery hopes to bring the MacDougall Trail up to hiking standards in the next few years.

Southwestern

Further Information: The complex offers an interpretive brochure to the Fraser's Trail. Additional information about provincial forestry guidelines and silviculture programs is also available.

Whycocomagh Provincial Park

Length: 2.5 km (1.5 mi) return
Time: 1-1.5 hr
Type: walking paths
Rating (1-5): 2

Uses: hiking
Facilities: outhouses, water, picnic tables, benches, camping, firewood, cooking shelters

Gov't Topo Map: Whycocomagh 11 F/14
Trailhead GPS Reference: N 45° 57" 58.7' W 61° 06" 18.2'

Access Information: The entrance to Whycocomagh Provincial Park is on the southeast (Sydney) side of Whycocomagh. Turn left off the highway at the signed road; the trailhead is just before the campground entrance opposite the Department of Natural Resources district office.

Introduction: Although it's the shortest hike found in this book, this is a walk that no one should overlook. The extraordinary view of Whycocomagh Bay and St. Patricks Channel from Salt Mountain justifies its inclusion. Do not be deceived by its short length, however, for the summit is 230 m (750 ft) above Bras d'Or Lake, requiring a steep climb indeed. Another attractive feature is the abundance of bald eagles in the Skye River Valley and Whycocomagh Bay. Good nesting locations and a plentiful fish supply in the lake mean that visitors will often sight an eagle soaring on the updrafts

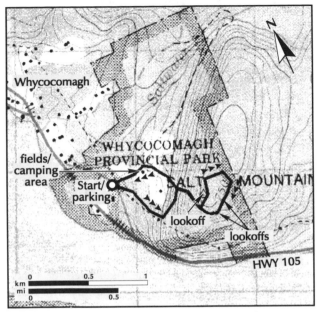

Whycocomagh Provincial Park

near the mountain or perching on a tree near the lake-shore.

Meaning "Head of the Waters," Whycocomagh is the Mi'kmaq word for the area surrounding Salt Mountain, and a large community of Native people lives across the bay from the park. Settled in 1812 by Highland Scots, the new community retained its original name despite the colonists' nostalgic fondness for reminders of their past, as Cape Breton place-names such as Glencoe, Skir Dhu, and Loch Lomond suggest. The 204-ha (504-a) park contains 62 campsites, a picnic area, and a boat launch. The property was donated to the Province of Nova Scotia in 1959 by Isabelle Stewart Farley, of Boston, in memory of her brother, Hugh McLellan, of Sydney, killed in World War I.

This is a short but challenging walk, and a good one for families. Ideal for campers at the park, this trail's proximity to the main road makes it a pleasant diversion for those passing by who want to stretch their legs and enjoy a marvellous view. Expect to earn it, however, by walking this steep trail.

Trail Description: The path starts broad and grassy with a wide entrance. Wooden arrows point along a well-defined path that begins to climb immediately. Crossing rocky ground, it gets a little rough. Notice the old stone wall on your right, evidence of earlier farming in the crofter style. Soon Whycocomagh Bay becomes visible on your right through the leaves, the slope so precipitous that you are soon higher than the tops of most trees on the hillside.

Switching back to the left, the route levels for a short distance. Note the stonework underfoot; this is a beautifully maintained trail. At a junction, an Exit sign points down the hill, while arrows continue to point up. A bench is provided for both the undecided and the weary. If you are already exhausted, you should consider returning down the hill after a brief rest. More strenuous activity is required in the remaining hike to the summit.

A second intersection soon after the first is also clearly marked, its arrows directing left. A series of short switchbacks takes you through another rough section, but then the trail becomes less steep. Nearing the summit, numerous side paths branch out, but the main trail remains quite distinct. The reward for your hard climb is a grassy clearing covering a rocky outcrop which faces west, overlooking Whycocomagh and the campground, a tremendous sight. Continuing on, climb a little more and loop around to the south side of Salt Mountain. On this side your view is of Orangedale and Marble Mountain. After you have spent enough time enjoying the panorama, follow the trail downhill. Just past this second lookoff is a bronze plaque set in granite and commemorating the donation of the park. After that, a final lookoff is situated on your left just before the path begins its steep descent.

Quickly you return to the intersections you passed on the way up. It's amazing how easy the trip downhill is, don't you think? Following the Exit sign leads you down a short, steep slope into the campground behind sites 82 and 83. You will notice that there are signs telling campers where to find the trailhead, but the exit here is somewhat camouflaged by thick foliage. The camping area is a gorgeous site located on the gentle slope of Salt Mountain with a view of the surrounding hills. To return to the car, follow the road downhill through the park to the administration building at the entrance. The parking area for the trail is to the left about 100 m/yd.

Cautionary Notes: Although short, the hike is quite steep with extended climbs. Take it easy on the way up, especially if you are a novice. People with mobility problems will find this hike extremely difficult if not impossible.

There are at least four different methods of signage used: flagging tape, black arrows on white signs, old metal signs with the hiker symbol, and varnished wood slices with burnt-in lettering. All should be heeded.

Some of the fences at the lookoffs were down in 1998; be cautious near the edge.

Cell Phone Coverage: Coverage is excellent throughout. I could find no dead spots.

Future Plans: A community group is planning to extend the path over the top of Salt Mountain to Saltwater Brook, creating both an easier walk from the campground and a longer day-hike.

Southwestern

Further Information: A brochure about the park is printed by the Nova Scotia Department of Natural Resources, and is available from the Parks and Recreation Division.

AFTERWORD

Perhaps what most surprised me about my experiences in Cape Breton was not that the beauty was spectacular, but that I could find so many locations that were so attractive. One might suspect that after a few coastal hikes, for example, a certain acceptance of the scenery would occur. After all, how different can one beach look from another? Yet consistently, week after week, I would discover another exciting path that captured my imagination. Friends and co-workers patiently endured detailed descriptions of the latest findings, only to have me come back a week later with a new site and another place that they "must see."

Inevitably, someone asks me which is my favourite trail. They understandably think that there is one particular location so sensational that it stands out among all the many possibilities. Whenever this happens, I always hesitate, and I usually reply vaguely that my choice depends on the time of year or some similar factor. In fact, I have no one favourite hike, unless maybe it is the last one I completed. But I can say this: I enjoy no scenery anywhere in the world more than that which I find on Cape Breton Island, and I have found no other place where I can consistently discover sites of such captivating beauty around virtually every corner. The people living on Cape Breton are extremely fortunate to be surrounded by this landscape, and I strongly recommend that all Islanders, mainlanders, and other Maritimers learn more about what exists in their own back yard.

I have described the hikes as I found them in the

summer and fall of 1998, but trails change over time, and more routes are being added every year, especially with initiatives such as the Trans Canada Trail underway. Discrepancies will occur more frequently with old roads and hikes outside parks, as logging, development, and even nature alter the landscape. Do not be discouraged if you find things a little different than described in *Hiking Trails of Cape Breton*. As long as you have map and compass, exploration can be half the fun.

I hope you enjoy the hikes found in these pages, and that they encourage you to add more outdoor activities to your life. If you have a path that you think should be included or are curious about one of the trails I have described, contact me through the Nova Scotia Trails Federation.

USEFUL ADDRESSES

Canadian Hostelling
   Association-Nova Scotia
PO Box 3010 South
Halifax NS B3J 3G6
(902) 425-5450

Environment Canada -
   Canadian Wildlife Service
PO Box 6227
Sackville NB E4L 1G6
(506) 364-5044

Cape Breton Regional
   Municipality Recreation
320 Esplanade
Sydney NS B1P 1A7
(902) 563-5513

Cape Breton Highlands
   National Park
Ingonish Beach NS B0C 1L0
(902) 285-2671

Cape Breton Island
   Hoppers (hiking club)
70 Tain Street
Sydney NS B2N 5H9
(902) 539-2823

Cape Mabou Trail Club
c/o Ian Sherman
Inverness NS B0E 1N0
(902) 258-2848

Extension Services
Dept. of Natural Resources
PO Box 698
Halifax NS B3J 2T9
(902) 424-4321

Inverness County Tourism Dept.
PO Box 179
Port Hood NS B0E 2W0
(902) 787-2274

Les Amis du Plein Air
PO Box 472
Cheticamp NS B0E 1H0
(902) 224-2306

Nature Conservancy of Canada
PO Box 8505
Halifax NS B3K 5M2
(902) 443-1080

Cross Country Ski
   Nova Scotia
PO Box 3010 South
Halifax NS B3J 3G6
(902) 425-5450 ext. 316

Nova Scotia Museum
   of Natural History
1747 Summer Street
Halifax NS B3H 3A6
(902) 424-7353

Nova Scotia Trails Federation
PO Box 3010 South
Halifax NS B3J 3G6
(902) 425-5450 ext. 325

Parks and Recreation Division
Dept. of Natural Resources
R.R.#1
Belmont NS B0M 1C0
(902) 662-3030

Port Hawkesbury
  Recreation Dept.
PO Box 10
Port Hawkesbury NS
B0E 2V0
(902) 625-2591

Richmond County
  Recreation Dept.
PO Box 120
Arichat NS B0E 1A0
(902) 226-2400

Development Isle Madame Ltd.
PO Box 57
Arichat B0E 1A0
(902) 226-1918

Route 223 Forest
  Management Co-op
R.R.#2, Box 17
Iona NS B0A 1L0
(902) 725-2061

Stora Enso Port Hawkesbury Ltd.
PO Box 59
Port Hawkesbury NS
B0E 2V0
(902) 625-2460 ext. 161

Tourism Cape Breton
PO Box 1448
Sydney NS B1P 6R7
1-800-565-9464

Victoria County
  Recreation Dept.
PO Box 370
Baddeck NS B0E 1B0
(902) 295-3231

BIBLIOGRAPHY

For many people, the popular field guides to birds, plants, animals, rocks and minerals, and geology of Eastern North America will provide sufficient knowledge about their surroundings. However, there is an increasing body of excellent local publications covering all of these areas that give more specific data and contribute to a substantially enriching experience for both the weekend walker and the more serious hiker. I have found that the more I read, the more I recognize how little I know about our natural surroundings. I particularly recommend the recently re-released *Natural History of Nova Scotia*.

The following list includes some of the texts I used for research for my hikes, but it omits all of the brochures, management plans, and other similar documents that were, at times, invaluable to my studies. In addition to the written materials, there were many conversations that proved as helpful as any book. I acknowledge my debt to them all.

Beardmore, R.M. 1985. *Atlantic Canada's Natural Heritage Areas*. Canadian Government Publishing Centre, Ottawa.

Billard, Allan. 1997. *Waterfalls of Nova Scotia*. Sand Dollar, Halifax.

Brown, Geoff and Kermit De Gooyer. 1996. *Mountain Bike Nova Scotia*. Nimbus, Halifax.

Cape Breton County Recreation Commission. *Trackdown: Trails in Cape Breton County*. Sydney.

Cape Breton Development Corporation. 1975. *Walk Cape Breton*. Sydney.

Claridge, E. and B. A. Milligan.1992. *Animal Signatures*. Nimbus and Nova Scotia Museum, Halifax.

Cunningham, Scott. 1996. *Sea Kayaking in Nova Scotia*. Nimbus, Halifax.

Davis, D.S. 1987. *Natural History Map of Nova Scotia*. Nova Scotia Museum and Department of Education, Halifax.

Davis, D.S., and S. Browne. 1996. *The Natural History of Nova Scotia*. Nimbus, Nova Scotia Museum, and Communications Nova Scotia, Halifax. 2 vol.

Donahoe, H.V. and R.G. Grantham. 1994. *Nova Scotia Geology Map*. Land Registration and Information Service and Department of Supply and Services. Halifax.

Erskine, J. 1971. *In Forest and Field*. Nova Scotia Museum, Halifax.

Gilhen, J. 1971. *Amphibians and Reptiles of Nova Scotia*. Nova Scotia Museum, Halifax.

Grant, D.R. 1988. *Surficial Geology, Cape Breton Island, Nova Scotia*. Geological Survey of Canada, Ottawa.

Lawley, David. 1994. *A Nature and Hiking Guide to Cape Breton's Cabot Trail*. Nimbus, Halifax.

Logue, Victoria. 1993. *Backpacking in the '90s*. Menasha Ridge, Birmingham, Alabama.

Nordic Ski Nova Scotia. 1993. *Nova Scotia Nordic Ski Trails*. Halifax.

Nova Scotia Bird Society. 1976. *Where to Find the Birds in Nova Scotia*. Halifax.

Nova Scotia Departments of Fisheries, Tourism, and Lands and Forests. 1987. *Fishing Guide to Nova Scotia*. Halifax.

Nova Scotia Department of Lands and Forests. 1980. *Notes on Nova Scotia Wildlife*. Truro.

Nova Scotia Department of Natural Resources. 1992. *A Map of the Province of Nova Scotia, Canada*. Formac, Halifax.

O'Neil, Pat. 1994. *Explore Cape Breton: A Field Guide to Adventure*. Nimbus, Halifax.

Public Archives of Nova Scotia. 1974. *Place-Names and Places of Nova Scotia*. Mika, Belleville.

Roland, A.E. 1982. *Geological Background and Physiography of Nova Scotia*. Nova Scotian Institute of Science, Halifax.

Roland, A.E. and E.C. Smith. 1969. *Flora of Nova Scotia*. Nova Scotia Museum, Halifax.

Roland, A.E. and A.R. Olsen.1993. *Spring Wildflowers*. Nimbus and Nova Scotia Museum, Halifax.

Saunders, G.L. 1970. *Trees of Nova Scotia*. Nova Scotia Department of Lands and Forests, Halifax.

Tufts, R. 1986. *Birds of Nova Scotia* (3rd edition). Nimbus and Nova Scotia Museum, Halifax.

ACKNOWLEDGEMENTS

I must begin by thanking my wife, Andrea Moritz, for her patience and support. When I wrote *Hiking Trails of Nova Scotia*, 7th Edition, I was single and could devote whatever ridiculous hours were required to complete the project. I had no idea what a bizarre lifestyle I was leading until this poor woman was required to share it. The fact that we are still married is a testament to her resilience, grace, and depth of affection. I appreciate all those fine qualities, and so many others that I see every day. Having her support made this an easier book to write (despite my need to behave normally occasionally).

MTT Mobility accepted the plan of including a description of cell phone coverage for each trail eagerly, and could not have provided greater support for my efforts. I wish to thank the company for supplying cellular service, and Downeast MTT Mobility for supplying the equipment. I also especially wish to thank Gary Nymark, whom I first approached with the idea and who supported it immediately, and Peter Landers, who kept offering me more and bigger phones.

Navitrak Engineering listened to my request to borrow a GPS receiver and immediately volunteered to supply the maps for the book. Michelle MacDonald and Rick MacDonald both made themselves available whenever I needed help with the technical data, and they provided valuable suggestions on using the satellite data. In the end, they let me monopolize a section of their office for a full day so I could draw the rough maps. Their mapping software permitted me to calculate distances very accurately.

Goose Lane Editions has been very supportive of this project, as they were with *Hiking Trails of Nova Scotia*. It has been a pleasure to work with Susanne Alexander, Laurel Boone, Ryan Astle, Ray Cronin, and all the others who transformed my rough ideas into something the public can use. Darrell Mesheau, the editor, deserves a special vote of thanks for his efforts in wading through the first draft and apparently maintaining his sanity.

Thanks are deserved by my employers: the Nova Scotia Trails Federation, the Nova Scotia Underwater Council, and the Orienteering Association of Nova Scotia, who had to work with my juggling a full-time job and a full-time project simultaneously.

Many people helped me find information, often about specific trails: Dave Alexander, Terry Campbell, Jody Conrad, John Cotton, Patricia Dietz, Sean Drohan, Darrell Landry, Anita MacLeod, Al MacDonald, Heather MacDougall, Burton MacIntyre, Karen Malcolm, D.B. Morrison, Irving Schwartz, Ted Scrutton, Ian Sherman, Stan Slack, and Darlene Sponagle are but a few.

I know I have missed naming some who should be mentioned. Please accept my apologies. This book would not be what it is without all your contributions. Thank you.

Michael Haynes
May, 1999

INDEX

TRAIL NOTES

TRAIL NOTES

TRAIL NOTES

TRAIL NOTES

TRAIL NOTES

TRAIL NOTES

ALSO AVAILABLE from Goose Lane Editions

Hiking Trails of Nova Scotia, 7th Edition

MICHAEL HAYNES

Hostelling International - Nova Scotia's definitive guide, featuring more than 60 hiking experiences and more than 800 km of trails.

0-86492-165-9 / $14.95 pb
1995 / 240pp / 4.25 x 7.25
maps, photographs, index, bibliography

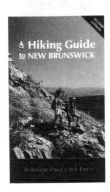

A Hiking Guide to New Brunswick, 2nd Edition

MARIANNE & H.A. EISELT

The updated edition of the Eiselts' indispensable guide to more than 90 hiking trails in New Brunswick, including maps, trail descriptions and photographs.

0-86492-188-8 / $12.95 pb
1996 / 320pp / 4.25 x 7.25
maps, photographs, index, bibliography

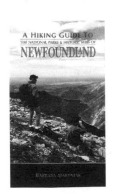

A Hiking Guide to the National Parks and Historic Sites of Newfoundland

BARBARA MARYNIAK

An enchanting and informative guide to more than 50 trails in Newfoundland's national parks and historic sites; includes maps and trail descriptions.

0-86492-150-0 / $12.95 pb
1994 / 320pp / 4.25 x 7.25
maps, photographs, index, bibliography

Trails of Fredericton
BILL THORPE

As well as being a guide to groomed paths and nature walks, *Trails of Fredericton* conveys the essence of this beautiful little city in historical vignettes, anecdotes, and photographs.

0-86492-235-3 / $12.95 pb
1999 / 120pp / 4.25 x 7.25
maps, photographs, index

Woodlands Canoeing: Pleasure Paddling on Woodland Waterways
RICK SPARKMAN

The fundamentals of recreational canoeing on woodland waterways, where the channels are narrow, the water is swift and canoeing changes with the seasons.

0-86492-234-5 / $16.95 pb
1998 / 200pp / 6 x 9 / illustrated

Weeds of the Woods: Small Trees and Shrubs of the Eastern Forest
GLEN BLOUIN

A full-colour identification guide that includes Latin names, common names in various languages, and information on ornamental, practical and medicinal uses.

0-86492-127-6 / $14.95 pb
1992 / 125pp / 6 x 9
colour photographs, index

Safe and Sound:
How Not to Get Lost in the Woods
and How to Survive If You Do

GORDON SNOW

No one expects to get lost — until it happens. *Safe and Sound* is full of survival tips, common sense preparations and advice from a veteran Mountie with more than 200 rescues to his credit.

0-86492-222-1 / $9.95 pb
1997 / 84pp / 4.25 x 7 / illustrated

Biking to Blissville:
A Cycling Guide to
the Maritimes and
the Magdalen Islands

KENT THOMPSON

A delightful and trustworthy cyclist's companion to 35 scenic rides in Maritime Canada.

0-86492-154-3 / $14.95 pb
1993 / 178pp / 6 x 9
maps, index

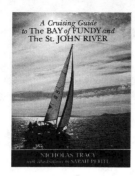

A Cruising Guide to the Bay of Fundy and the St. John River

NICHOLAS TRACY
Illustrated by SARAH PETITE

An informative guide to sailing the Bay of Fundy, the St. John River, Passamaquoddy Bay and the southwestern shore of Nova Scotia.

0-86492-129-2 / $29.95 spiral bound
1992 / 200pp / 8 x 10
illustrated, charts, index

To order these books contact your local bookseller or:

GOOSE LANE EDITIONS
469 King Street
Fredericton, NB
Canada   E3B 1E5
Toll Free: 1 (888) 926 8377
Fax: (506) 459 4991
e-mail: gooselane@nb.aibn.com